THE WESTERN HORSE
Advice and Training

THE WESTERN HORSE
Advice and Training
by
Dave Jones

UNIVERSITY OF OKLAHOMA PRESS
Norman and London

By Dave Jones

Practical Western Training (New York, 1966)
The Western Horse: Advice and Training (Norman, 1974)
The Western Trainer (New York, 1976)

Library of Congress Cataloging-in-Publication Data
Jones, Dave, 1927–
  The western horse.
  SUMMARY: Advises aspiring trainers on the techniques and prob-
lems of buying, breeding, and handling horses.
  1. Horse—training. 2. Horse buying.
  [1. Horses—Training] I. Title.
SF287.J62 1974   636.1'0886   73–7422
  ISBN: 0–8061–2334–6

    6   7   8   9   10   11   12   13   14   15   16   17   18   19   20

Contents

Illustrations

THE WESTERN HORSE
Advice and Training

1 *Advice to a Young Person Who Has a Burning Desire to Be a Trainer*

Many young people, boys and girls, write to me because they can think of nothing they'd rather do than make a career for themselves as horse trainers. They ask my advice and hint broadly for my help. I always answer their letters and give them the best advice I can.

I'm pleased that these young people think enough of me as a trainer to ask my advice pertaining to their futures. The best advice I can give them is to make training an avocation rather than a vocation. Do something else for a living, and train horses as a hobby.

The apprenticeship is long in this business, because you should never stop trying to learn more about horses and a better way to train them. A great many of yesterday's and today's trainers have learned a little bit and they think they know a lot. Few have learned that there are many trails, different ways, to reach the same goal, a highly trained horse. They have learned how to hit a horse over the head and stick a spur in his shoulder. There's more to horse training than this.

Ideally the apprentice trainer should have a lot of money so that he could sit at the feet of the many great trainers in the different parts of the country and the world. He would spend a year in Texas, a few years in California. Perhaps he might spend some of his money learning from the masters of dressage in this country. This would whet his appetite, and he'd travel to Europe to learn from the best there.

Still different means of training are practiced in Spain where the horse must learn to outmaneuver the fighting bulls. The apprentice could learn how to do this, and the information would be very valuable in the future.

Horses are trained by different means in each of the countries of South America. The gaucho of Argentina has his methods. The *amansador* of Colombia has training methods that have been handed down for centuries. The *jinete* of Peru also knows his business, and some time should be spent with him.

After all the expense and traveling, the apprentice would come up with a few basic facts. First, he'd learn that all these different methods produce the same result, a trained horse. He'd find that opinions vary about what a trained horse is. The gaucho would believe the Peruano to be a stupid fool, a "tonto" who knows nothing about horses. The dressage expert would shudder at the crude horses every one else passes off as finished, while the ole' salt would snicker at the dressage trainer for spending five years to teach a horse what "he could do in a week with a set of hooks and a shot-loaded quirt."

The whole point I'm making is that a trainer, to be a good one, should work in different places to learn his craft, picking the minds of the top trainers from each area. He might be a success by learning his trade in one place and practicing his trade in the same place. This is fine if you're honest about it. If you think the best training is to be found in Texas, go there to learn your craft. If the Spanish riding school is your goal as the ultimate product, that's the place to try.

I'm disgusted with people who think that their kind of horse, gear, and methods of horse handling are the ultimate and only way. My acquaintances in the stock-horse world ridicule an English saddle and call it a "pancake" or "postage stamp." People who ride English think anyone using a stock saddle isn't worth noticing. I know a woman who thinks that anyone who uses any bit other than a snaffle is a barbarian.

You have gathered by now that I think a trainer should have an open mind. If he can train a reining horse by using a dressage saddle and Weymouth bridle, I'm for him. It's results that count.

I've been lucky and unlucky, I guess. Working for an outfit in this part of the country and another in that part of the country has given me a broad outlook and an open mind. It would be tough if I had a large family.

If a trainer could always work for the perfect ranch owner and ride top horses, life would be pleasant. I'd say, "Go to it." But horse owners are a peculiar lot, and the business is tricky. You will seldom find *the* top trainer at *the* best outfit.

A businessman decides that horse raising might be a profitable business. A short period of investigation leads him to thoughts such as these: "I can buy a mare for $2500. I can breed her and sell her colt for $1500. She's free with her second colt. I don't know where I could invest money to show a more profitable return."

He then proceeds to buy a ranch (or farm) and some mares. He generally buys poor-quality stock and pays a premium. His trainer-manager faces problems when he starts. Generally, he can't sell the colts for enough money to pay his own salary. A few years of this and the horse owner quits. The trainer needs a new job.

And the trainer needs a job *now*. He didn't make enough money to allow him to wait until a good job appears. He must take what's available. The trainer who, in January,

5

1971, was managing the top stable in Wyoming might, in July, 1974, find himself riding five plugs, living in a two-room shack, making $125 a month in a little town in, say, Georgia. Most trainers could give you a real tale of woe about such happenings.

So what happens when a trainer finds himself in such a spot? He keeps in touch the best way he can to get out. When a good job opens up, he tries to be first in line with a fistful of references. Of course, trainers get the reputation for being "fiddle-footed." This is why. Give a good trainer a *good* job and he'll be there a long time.

I'm married but have no children. I always feel sorry for a decent trainer who has a large family when he gets trapped. Many good horsemen have to stay put for security. They can't go rambling on in search of a better job. They must take what's there and make it do.

If I'm training for an outfit where things are unsuitable, I quit. Peace of mind is important to me. I've had my own training business in different places, and there's many a pitfall to that, too.

I moved to Tallahassee, Florida, a few years ago and started my own little business. I was the only trainer in the region, and before long business was pretty good. I even had to enlarge the barn I built and leased. It was a nice, quiet, fulfilling life. I was training horses, and I was putting a little money in the bank.

Then one day a fellow visited me who wanted to train horses in Florida. He'd been working in the North and was sick of cold winters. He managed to get a toehold. Then another arrived—and another. These guys saw that I was making a living, and they thought they could too. Soon there were five or six men in the locality, an area that could only ade-

6

quately support one trainer. Prices dropped lower and lower in a price war to get horses. Soon no one could make it.

I saw the handwriting on the wall and relocated, joining a big horse outfit as manager-trainer. It was a good job, and the timing was right. Now, after a few years with this big outfit, I have again started my own business.

Really, what's happening to trainers has a direct relationship to what's happening to farming and ranching activities. Large land areas, farms, and ranches are being broken up for homesites. Land is getting too valuable to use as pasture for horses and cattle. If this trend continues, it will spell doom to large ranches and farms in the near future. Oh, sure, there'll be pleasure horses. Horses will need training, and some trainers will make a living. But I do think the life of a trainer won't be as nice as it has been.

So, my advice still goes. I recommend training as an avocation, not a vocation. But if you must be a trainer, I suggest the following.

1. Stay single or, at least, don't raise a family, unless you have a private income. You should be able to move.

2. Don't own land. With land you tie yourself down to one locality. If business gets bad, you must stay on your land. With no ties, moving is possible.

3. Learn how others do it. Move around when you have the chance. Pick a top trainer's brain, and move to a different section of the country. Don't be afraid to learn something different. Top trainers of western horses are learning that there's a strong similarity between the top reining horses and dressage horses. More advanced methods are being used by the best. Be the best!

4. Keep flexible. Think ahead. Think. Reason. Figure out the angles, and plan your moves. Read. Listen. Keep an open mind. Don't criticize methods other than your own. Rather, learn the other methods.

5. Be able to change. I knew a trainer who was terrible when riding a stock saddle, but he had to show horses in both western and English gear. His cutting horses feared him and worked in poor fashion. His reining horses were high-headed nothings. But he was a winner when riding English. Still, he couldn't reason it out that he should train and show English. If you know just one way to train horses, have just one method, follow an inflexible style, you'll be able to train some horses. You'll say, "This is a good colt. He can do it." But you'll find another colt that won't respond to your "one-track" methods, and you'll say, "Come get this colt. He isn't going to make it." Heck, he might make it at almost anything, but you wanted a horse to follow your narrow guidelines.

6. The financial aspects are better for the versatile trainer. If you move to a town where there's no trainer, you might get almost all the colts raised in the vicinity if you'll train English *and* western, doing a good job at both.

II Advice about Buying Horses

The question of buying horses should be taken up in parts. If the animals are to be pleasure horses for family riding, fewer miles need to be covered in the search. But if future sales are to be considered, or if buying horses to start a horse business is the aim, many points need to be taken up.

Let's take pleasure horses first. There are a great many breed organizations today, and there are great numbers of pleasure horses in the United States. Do spots appeal to you? A variety of Appaloosas and paints await your desire and checkbook. Is the popular Quarter Horse your goal? Buy now. You'll have little trouble finding good ones. Does the sight of a proud Arabian horse send chills up and down your spine? Plenty are available. Want an ultrasmooth ride? There are fine Pasos from Colombia, Puerto Rico, and Peru waiting to be purchased.

The horses are here. A very easy way to check them out is to obtain a copy of the annual October issue of the *Western Horseman Magazine*. This is the "All-Breeds" issue, and the association addresses are listed in the back. There are write-ups about many breeds in this issue, so information is readily available. A letter to the association office should bring you additional information and a list of breeders. The address for the magazine is: *Western Horseman*, 3850 North Nevada Ave., Colorado Springs, Colorado 80901.

I think the personal pleasure horse should be a gentle

gelding and a good representative of his breed. Conformation of the western horse can be generally described as a pleasing appearance. The head should be refined, with plenty of width between the eyes. The eyes should be large and tranquil, and the ears should be small and sharply pointed. I prefer a neck that is refined and fairly long. The withers should be prominent, but not so high as to make the purchase of a special saddle necessary. The horse should have a fairly deep girth, and the underline shouldn't show a steep cut up to the flank; that is, the horse should be deep through the loin. Legs should appear sturdy with enough bone to support the horse's weight. The hind legs should be neither too crooked nor too straight. Check the diagram in the accompanying illustration for this. The front legs should appear slightly knock-kneed when viewed from the front. Bench knees are to be avoided; again check the diagram. Hoofs should be neither too small nor too large. The large "paddle-footed" horse isn't desirable, but the hoof should be large enough for adequate support.

Ride the prospective pleasure horse, and look for certain things. Can he easily be legged up into a lope? I hope he doesn't carry an extremely high head. He should stop without popping his head up. The nose should come in, not up. He should walk away on a loose rein.

The walk is often neglected. Many horses have such a slow walk that they are never a pleasure. The walk should be free and eager. Nothing will wear a rider out sooner than trying to leg a horse up to a fast walk when the horse is by nature a "poke-along." This is why the cowboy says, "I'd rather have a fresh horse than a meal." A horse is no pleasure if he doesn't have a good walk.

Ride enough horses to know what a good trot and canter (or lope) are. If your horse beats you to death with a hard trot and rough canter, you've made a bad buy. You should easily be able to set a trot for an hour if you're in condition. If the horse "crabs" at a lope, he'll tire you out. A "crabbing" horse lopes with his head pointed a bit away from his lead. If he's in his left lead, his head (and whole body) will point to the right, and you'll notice that your left stirrup is a foot farther forward than your right. This lope is twisting and very uncomfortable.

I'd lope this horse in circles, both ways, to check his leads, which should be taken freely. If he carries his head far to the right when in a left lead, his training is poor. I wouldn't consider this a major fault if everything else seems all right. I'd retrain the horse.

The horse should back easily and straight. I wouldn't ask him to back more than five steps. The trained horse should find this easy. However, if his backing up is poor but he still tries, I'd O.K. him and work on this aspect of his education. But if he refuses or rears, forget it. If the horse makes any attempt to rear, I'd look for another horse. A horse with such an inclination is a dangerous animal.

After the horse has trotted and loped for fifteen minutes, stop him and see if he'll walk away on a loose rein. If he won't do this, you know you'll have trouble getting him to settle down. It's no fun forcing a horse to walk when he wants to run.

Finally, I'd ride the horse some distance from the barn, stop, and see if he'll walk back on a loose rein. If he won't do this, he has a case of "barn-sour," which is generally difficult to correct. A barn-sour horse is never a pleasure.

If your prospect passes the conformation and riding tests and is the kind of horse you want, the last obstacle is the price. Shopping around should tell you whether or not the animal's price is competitive. Don't let a few dollars deter

PARTS OF A HORSE

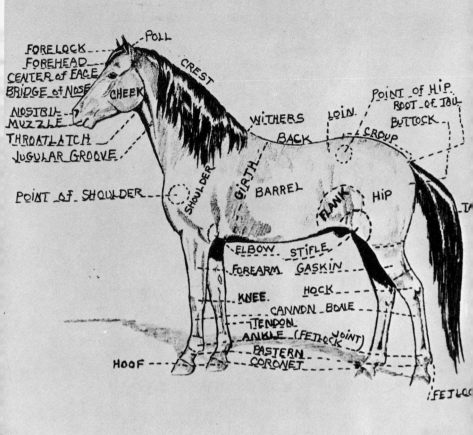

The parts of a horse.

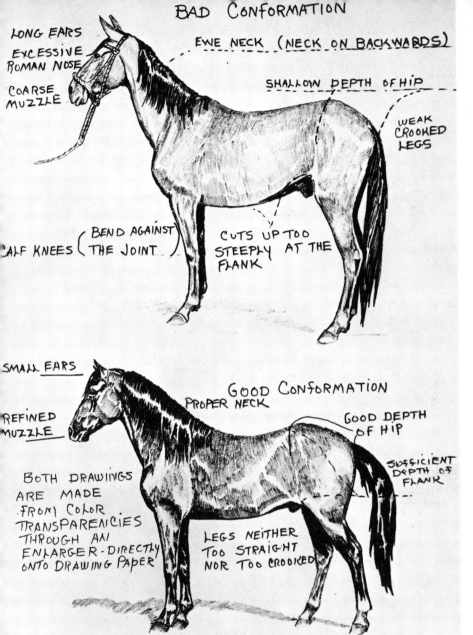

BAD CONFORMATION

LONG EARS

EXCESSIVE ROMAN NOSE

COARSE MUZZLE

EWE NECK (NECK ON BACKWARDS)

SHALLOW DEPTH OF HIP

WEAK CROOKED LEGS

CALF KNEES (BEND AGAINST THE JOINT)

CUTS UP TOO STEEPLY AT THE FLANK

SMALL EARS

REFINED MUZZLE

GOOD CONFORMATION

PROPER NECK

GOOD DEPTH OF HIP

SUFFICIENT DEPTH OF FLANK

BOTH DRAWINGS ARE MADE FROM COLOR TRANSPARENCIES THROUGH AN ENLARGER - DIRECTLY ONTO DRAWING PAPER

LEGS NEITHER TOO STRAIGHT NOR TOO CROOKED

Good and poor conformation.

13

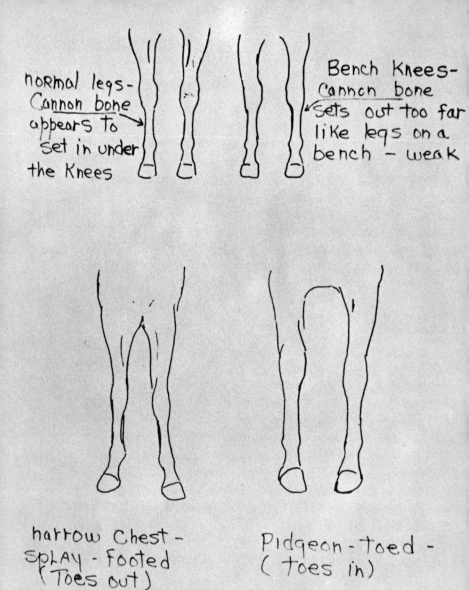

normal legs-
Cannon bone
appears to
set in under
the Knees

Bench Knees-
Cannon bone
sets out too far
like legs on a
bench - weak

narrow chest -
SPLAY - footed
(Toes out)

Pidgeon - toed -
(toes in)

Normal legs: cannon bone appears to set in under the knees. Bench
knees: cannon bone sets out too far, like the legs on a bench. Narrow
chest and splayfooted (toes out). Pigeon-toed (toes in).

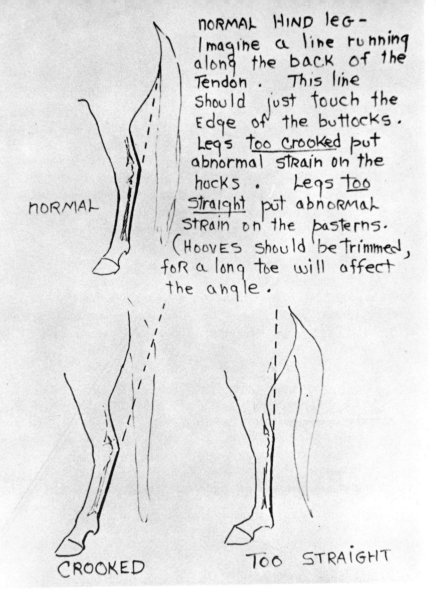

NORMAL HIND leg -
Imagine a line running
along the back of the
Tendon. This line
should just touch the
edge of the buttocks.
Legs too crooked put
abnormal strain on the
hocks. Legs too
straight put abnormal
strain on the pasterns.
(Hooves should be trimmed,
for a long toe will affect
the angle.

NORMAL

CROOKED   TOO STRAIGHT

The hind leg. Imagine a line running along the back of the tendon. This line should just touch the edge of the buttocks. Legs too crooked put abnormal strain on the hocks; legs too straight put too much strain on the pasterns. Because a long toe will affect this angle, the hoofs should be kept trimmed.

15

A horse with a fine head and a generally good conformation. He is Criol, a young Paso stallion by Mahoma out of Salpicada.

you, for the well-trained horse with good conformation should bring a premium.

There are a few more points to ponder if you're buying horses to start a business. Taking some time to consider all the aspects of your horse business might make the difference between profit and loss, between folding up or having a good business.

Quarter Horses are very popular in certain localities. Generally a business should be good where you have large cities and many shows. Texas is home for the Quarter Horse and has more shows for this breed of horse than any other state. A Quarter Horse business located near Houston or Dallas should do pretty well.

Still, popular bloodlines are important. The "bull-dog" style Quarter Horse isn't popular now. Middle-of-the-road to Thoroughbred type is what's selling, so this is the type to raise.

It is necessary to have a good location, pleasing facilities, popular bloodlines, top conformation, and well-trained animals. Get these things, and business should be good.

I think the horse buyer should read everything available about the horse of his choice. He should subscribe to the magazine devoted to his breed. Read and dream. Visit horse farms and ranches to get an idea of what's for sale and how business is. Learn what a good typical animal is. Visit sales. Use mathematics to figure out whether you can make a profit or fold up with a loss. If Arabian horses can make a profit in your locality but Quarter Horses can't, I believe I'd raise Arabian horses or move. By figuring these things out in advance you greatly improve your chances.

17

III *Can Pleasure Horses Be Raised Profitably?*

Let's go into the method of operation in more detail. Say we have a good location, fine representatives of the breed, pleasant facilities, and well-trained individuals. Where do we go from here? How do we market offspring?

Advertise your horses. You do this by putting ads in magazines and by showing horses. Showing is first in importance. You must do this in order to get "propaganda" for your magazine ads.

Let's go back to location. If a proper location has been picked, you will be able to have a large number of shows which the public can easily reach. You must haul your horses to these shows and win. If you have the right horses, you'll win at the shows.

Naturally, you can't haul eighty horses to a show. You can haul two, three, or four. Many people show a nice profit by owning only a few horses and doing their own work of fitting, training, and showing. They keep overhead down by doing the work themselves. Salaries eat up profit. A small do-it-yourself operation is very feasible today.

For instance, let's say you buy two horses of good bloodlines and conformation for twenty-five hundred dollars apiece. You then fit and train these animals, keeping them long enough to take capital gains. During their training they can be shown at halter. This lets people know you have good stock, and it gets the horses used to hauling and the activity at the shows. When the horses are ready, you enter the events you think they'll excel in. It may take a certain period of time before you "acquire the winning habit," but if you have the right horses and show them to their best advantage, you'll soon have a roomful of ribbons and trophies.

You may have chances to sell your horses for a good profit at the shows. In any event, you'll have the necessary material for magazine advertisements. If you keep the number of your horses small and sell them for a good profit, you're coming out ahead. It's easier to find a couple of buyers for five-thousand-dollar horses than it is to find fifty buyers for cheaper animals.

You may want to start a real horse ranch. The same formula for success must be followed. Don't fall into the cheap-horse trap. You might sell a few cheap horses, but keeping it up year after year soon floods the market, and the cheap-horse market soon turns into no market. If you can't sell a colt for more money than it takes to raise him, you can easily figure out the results.

Quality must go along with quantity. If you have twenty brood mares, you must have twenty top brood mares. Like begets like. If your good mare doesn't produce a good colt, market her, for she's not a good mare.

You can make money with a few horses if you do your own work. If you hire help, you must have many more mares to pay for salaries and increased taxes from sales. You can handle four mares and a stallion with no help. Eight or nine mares won't pay for the extra expenses. You need to move up to fourteen to twenty mares or more. With increasing numbers of horses you need more help.

It's hard to find that many top mares. It's hard to find five top mares for sale. Much horse hunting is necessary, and a lot of reading and investigation is a must to know just what a top mare is. The months or years of searching pay dividends —a paying horse business.

Speed horses can also be pleasure horses. Speed bloodlines command more money. Arabians, Appaloosas, and Quarter Horses all have racing strains. By raising speed horses, your chances of success should be better. A pleasure and halter horse with top speed bloodlines should be readily marketable.

If you're a beginner and want to start a horse business, you have a tough row to hoe. You're going to get stuck if you blindly buy stock. Expert advice is misleading because your expert will want to sell you his horses or the horses of an associate. If I wanted to start a horse business for the first time, I'd proceed as follows.

First, I'd read everything available. Horse magazines and books would be my daily fare. At the same time I'd get to know a person who has a successful horse business and ask him for advice. I'd invite him to dinner and try to make him a good friend. If he'd let me ride his horses, I'd do so to find out what a winning horse is. I'd ask his advice about gear, trailers, showing and training methods, and anything else that would help me. I'd balance this information against what I'd learned from my reading.

I'd go to horse shows with this friend and help him in any way possible. I'd hold horses, clean horses, and help him load and unload. I'd help him around his stable. Maybe he'd let me exercise some old horse that he and his help didn't have time for. I'd ask his advice and be pleased with his criticisms, for he would be helping me learn. My labors should offset my eternal questions.

My next step would be to get a horse to show. A coming two-year-old filly would be a good choice. I'd try to exercise and fit her for the show ring myself. My buddy the showman would give me advice when it was needed.

Maybe my choice of animals would be poor. Maybe my buddy would sell me a horse not quite good enough to win. At any rate, it would be just one animal, not a herd. If I had to sell my choice at a loss, I wouldn't get hurt too badly. This is the way to learn.

When showing my horse, I'd ask others who are showing to give me their opinions. If they all agree, if they all fault my animal a certain way, I can certainly profit from their criticism. I might even ask a judge once in a while. When I went to the judge, I'd say, "Mr. Smith, I'm a rank amateur and sincerely want to learn what a good horse is. You didn't place my filly, and I'd like your personal opinion of her. I know you can't remember her out of all the vast numbers you're looking at, but I'd always be grateful if you'd take a quick squint at her if you have the time." I know of no judge who wouldn't help if he were asked in such a manner. Going up to a judge, ranting and raving, "Why the 'ell didn't you place my filly?" will get you nothing but a terrible reputation.

Maybe I place my filly at a few shows and start to get some experience. I'm learning how to take care of my horse and how to behave at a show. I'm learning why my filly is only placing a little and not winning them all. I'm starting to see the difference between a top animal and a mediocre one. One day a man comes up to me and says, "I've been watching your filly for quite a while. Seems a shame she's not placing better. I think she's better than the winner today, and I'd like to buy her."

This is pleasing information, and with a little negotiation, the filly changes hands. She's sold, and I'm out on top. Now's the time to look for the "top one."

So I start horse hunting. My experiences and reading have taught me much more about winning horses. I finally find

21

a filly that has top bloodlines and conformation. The price is high, but I buy her.

My new filly likes her home. Proper worming, feeding, blanketing, hoof trimming, and exercise soon have her blossoming. My training is paying off, for she wins her class at her first show. This is the first top one for me, and I continue my search for more of her kind.

This is the way a string of top animals should be put together. It might be possible to buy such a filly's dam and breed her back to the stallion that produces such a winner. The gradual accumulation of top animals will ensure the horseman a successful horse business. Raising winners means success. If you have *the* product, you'll have no trouble marketing it.

IV Possessive Pride

The thing that has held the horse business back—putting sorry horses on the market—is possessive pride—pride in what we own. The horse that is my personal property always looks better to me than other horses. The stallion will be uncastrated and used at stud even though he has glaring faults and passes them on. "His merits outweigh his faults," I say to myself, "and it'd be a terrible shame to geld such a fine animal." This kind of thinking has lowered the quality and the price of horses to such an extent that it's tough for anyone to make a living in the horse business.

It's a difficult thing to stand back, take a long look at your own horses, and say "They ain't much." Some people can do this. I've heard about horse owners who take this long look at their horses (even show winners) and tear up their papers, selling them as grade animals.

Let's say that a man has picked up five cheap mares. All five mares have been bred to a good (but not great) stallion. Four have produced fillies, and one has produced a colt. The colt's ears are long, but, he says, "You don't ride the ears." He's too narrow between the eyes, but he's so cute that this flaw is overlooked. The back legs are too crooked, but, he thinks, "We'll trim him right and he'll straighten up." The family loves this little horse, and when the time comes, they can't even think about castrating him. He's a hundred-dollar plug, but he's bred to four mares to whom he's not related. The resulting offspring are terrible, and the owner thinks the whole world's against him when he tries to sell them. Sure, they're registered, but they don't represent their breed. They're cheap plug horses. "I just can't seem to sell my colts," the owner wails. He can't get enough money for them to pay his feed bill.

This horseman has a friend. This friend reads in the *Wall Street Journal* that a brood mare is a great investment. He has a little land and decides to go into the horse business. Of course, he talks to his "horsy" friend.

Now this guy with the plug horses lights up like a Christmas tree. He describes his horses in glowing terms to "Mr. Prospective," who doesn't know a horse from a jackass, and sells him a bill of goods. The fledgling opens his checkbook, and he's in the horse business.

Boys, it's the end of a beautiful friendship. And a man who could have added a lot to the horse business writes the whole thing off as a loss, cancels his subscription to the *Wall Street Journal*, and hauls those plugs to a sale, where he loses his shirt.

This is how it happens more often than not. There must be huge numbers of people who would love to be in the horse business. Getting the hook at the first transaction drives them away from horses permanently. They're luckier than those who get suckered along for a number of years before getting the ax.

The breed associations have hindered rather than helped the problem by making registration so easy. A tough association is needed to keep breed quality high. The associations are all too prone to close the studbooks—which means inspection is over, and a numbered horse bred to a numbered mare gives you an automatically registered offspring. Just fill out an application, enclose your check, and you have a registered foal.

Not naming names, but it's been easy to get colts registered when they had to be inspected. Put the inspector up overnight, feed him well, turn on your friendly personality, and you had it made. Actually, all this buttering up wasn't needed. The inspector had seen so many "dinks" that registering a mediocre horse was a pushover.

Going a step farther, some breed associations have a half-bred registry. As if it's not bad enough registering sorry horses, the breed associations make it possible to breed a registered plug to a grade plug and get papers.

In defense the associations say that there's a weeding-out process when the good horses will sift to the top and the unworthy ones will fall to the bottom of the heap and peter out. Unfortunately, the newcomer to the business generally gets hooked with horses that are supposed to have been weeded out.

Now let's say that you have good horses. They're the top of the heap. You've paid through the nose for them and *must* get good prices. A prospective buyer, a beginner in the trade, shows up. You show him your horses and name their winnings. This horse has won here and there. His sons and daughters are big winners everywhere they go. All this goes well until the buyer asks the price.

He has a predictable reaction: "Why, So-and-So just down the road, has a great horse for $350. He priced all his mares to me for less than $400 apiece. Why should I pay $6,500 for one of your horses when his are just as good? His horses are all registered." And so it goes. The buyer just can't see why he should pay a large sum for one registered horse when he can buy another registered horse for a fraction of your asking price. He'll buy the cheap horse every time.

People who raise race horses have it in black and white. I think this may be better. If their horse can't run and win, if his offspring can't run and win, he's a plug horse. A race horse must be fast, and that kind brings big money.

So if you're a new horseman, go out and take a good long look at your horses. If you have any doubt about the prospects of your stallion, call your vet and tell him to fetch his knife. Haul your good mares to the best stallion you can find. Cull out the mediocre mares and get in the business the right way. If you must be sentimental, get that way about your top horses and get tough about the others.

V *Enjoying Your Horses*

I know many horse owners who might as well raise Persian cats for all the enjoyment they get from their horses. They feed and ride them, but the riding is misery instead of fun. Yet other people with the same facilities really enjoy their horses. Their riding horses are pleasant. They enjoy their horses.

Common sense makes the difference. The folks whose horses are never any fun just use the horses on weekends. They keep their animals on full feed and stand them in stalls Monday through Friday and expect a nice ride on the weekend. It can't be done.

A horse needs some daily exercise. Surplus energy must be worked off or the rider must contend with a spooky, broncy horse. Daily exercise is the difference between misery and enjoyment.

Take any highly trained horse, stand him in a stall all week, and he'll become unmanageable very quickly. Years of training can be undone instantly by people who don't consider the exercise factor.

Some folks are able to ride every day. They have no problem. A daily ride for an hour should keep the edge off any horse unless he's fed an overabundance of grain. A day of bad weather once in a while won't make that much difference. But it's often impossible for people to ride every day. Their horses need exercise and should have it provided. How can this be done?

27

One method is the exercise run. At Meridian Meadows, a stable in Tallahassee, Florida, which I managed for five years, all our stalls opened into a twenty-four by one-hundred-foot exercise run. The animals could take whatever exercise they wanted. Quite often they didn't take enough, but at least it was available to them. The expense of having such runs is high if you have a lot of horses. Since we boarded quite a number of pleasure horses, the stall occupants helped pay for the added expense.

We boarded horses for professional people, such as doctors and lawyers, who paid an additional fee for board with exercise. Their horses had an exercise run and were also ridden every other day or so. A telephone call to us the day before they wanted to ride would ensure them a horse that they could enjoy. The cost wasn't prohibitive, because it was only a third more than straight board. When a stable has enough horses to make such a plan pay, an extra exercise boy can be employed.

Quite often saddle horses can be turned out together in a pasture. True, there's a chance that your best saddle horse might get injured. If you have three horses, you might be able to turn only two out together. But you're getting two of the three exercised. You might want to turn them out only in the daytime and get them up at night. Remember, for the health of your horse and for your safety and pleasure, your horse needs daily exercise.

Don't turn your horse out in a pasture fenced with barbed wire unless you first put up a strand of electric wire. Any fence reinforced with electric wire teaches a horse to avoid the fence, the most dangerous part of your pasture. Check your pasture for poisonous plants. It's surprising how many there are, and it's more surprising how many horsemen are totally ignorant about them. For years I was among the totally ignorant and today am ashamed of my ignorance. Poisonous plants at Meridian Meadows included crotalaria, lantana, and deadly nightshade. Many trees are also poisonous to horses. Cherry trees and many citrus trees are of this group. Check with your county agent.

The poorly trained horse is never enjoyable, and the spoiled horse is a misery to ride. Sometimes it's a lot of fun to retrain your own animal if it has no extremely dangerous bad habits. To me, a barn-sour horse is a frustrating animal and needs retraining.

A mild case of this affliction can be tackled by the inexperienced horse owner if he knows what to do. You'll make your horse barn-sour if you run him to the barn or allow him to return to the barn at a faster pace than a flat-footed walk. You can cure him by forcing him to walk to the barn. Old confirmed bad-habit horses are almost impossible to cure. A newly acquired habit is fairly easy to reverse.

Walk him the last half mile back to the barn. When you get back, don't immediately turn him into his fine pasture or comfortable stall. Tie him up for a while so the return isn't too pleasant. Don't tire him too much. He'll enjoy the exercise if he's fresh. Carry a little feed or something he likes and feed him away from the barn. Make him like it away from the barn, and you're well on your way toward cure. Training problems will be gone into in detail later. Most bad habits can be corrected by following the instructions in this book.

A great deal of information is available for do-it-yourself training problems. I think Henry Wynmalen's books *Equitation* and *Dressage* are very good. The explanations in these books are fairly clear.

A horse is never out of training. A horse will pick up undesirable habits that you, as his owner, should straighten out. Most horses are terribly undertrained. They have had almost

29

no correct basic training, going from starting bit or hacka-more into a finishing bit in a matter of weeks, rather than years. If the horse is basically gentle, there's no reason why you can't begin again and educate your horse into a well-trained animal that will give you years of enjoyment.

You should be proud of your horse. This means that your horse should be registered and should be a fine example of his breed. A young horse can be retrained. An old, spoiled horse is impossible. If your hobby is sport cars, you certainly wouldn't be happy owning only an old jeep. The same with horses. Buy a good one and train him well.

Another piece of advice: don't buy cheap gear. I'd rather own a good twenty-year-old saddle than a cheap new one. A production-line saddle will fit neither you nor your horse. If you buy a Quarter Horse, buy a saddle to fit him. A special saddle for the Arabian will make work much more pleasant. Investigate before you buy; learn what is good by asking people in the business.

You can learn more about handling horses from books than you can from many old salts. Chances are they'll give you poor advice. Seek advice only from top professional horsemen. For instance, someone might tell you that alumi-num bits are the only decent bits for a horse because of their light weight. This fellow might have once had a horse he rode with an aluminum bit. He remembers the horse with affection because time makes the horses of the past perfect animals. But his advice is poor. Aluminum bits aren't good bits. Most horses hate the taste of such a bit and will sour in them. Any professional horseman will tell you this.

Learn how a good horse works and aim at that goal. Don't settle for less. Get a well-trained horse and buy good gear for him. Exercise him properly, ride him correctly, and you'll enjoy him.

VI *The Intelligence of the Horse*

I know that there are books on the subject of the intelligence of animals, and I find that horses are low on the list. According to very learned men, a horse might be a little smarter than a cow, but not much. To surprise everyone right now, I'm going to agree with these men Horses are pretty stupid —but we love them anyhow. And yet, I've seen horses do some very smart things—but heck, they're dumb.

I know of no other animal that will purposely stick a leg into a fence and then blindly fight to get it out. How many animals would catch their heads in a forked tree and hang themselves? Did you ever see two horses, friends, go through a gate? One horse might make it through the gate, but the other will charge up and down the fence, perhaps trying to jump it to go with his friend, while the open gate is only a few feet away. A mare might break through a pasture fence to join another mare and then get into a terrific fight with her friend.

Few horses show affection for their owners. They love their feed, their rewards, their nice stall, and so on, but they care little for humans. A horse might tear his stall up, eat his manger from boredom, and want exercise the worst way but will still storm and prance to get back to his stall when taken away from it.

Still it seems that the horse was designed for man's use. Too much intelligence would be hard to handle in such a

31

large animal. Imagine trying to doctor a horse with a dog's intelligence. Imagine trying to ride a big dog! A horse is a creature of habit, and man capitalizes on this trait when handling the horse.

A colt in training shouldn't be rushed; he shouldn't be given many new things to digest at a time. Each old routine must be rehashed to keep the performance habit strong. Only then is a new accomplishment added to the repertory.

The older horse, tired and weary, will still carry his rider mile after mile. The overridden cow horse will still give his all when his rider asks him to make a quick dash so an injured cow can be roped and doctored. This is habit.

The tired horse goes on and on because he's always done so. The cow horse knows that his rider is going to catch a cow when the rider unlimbers his lariat. The horse will run to rate (track) the cow because he's done so many times. Habit is a strong trait in a horse. It's what makes him useful to man.

Let's forget the *degree* of intelligence of the horse and think of him as an intelligent or a stupid animal. We'll say the horse that has a good head, learns his lessons rapidly, and retains what he learns is a very intelligent animal. The horse that has a bad head (is narrow between his little piggish eyes) and learns and retains little will be considered stupid.

Many years ago cow ranches used horses for everything. Bronc twisters were put on the payroll to start colts, and these salty men rode nothing but colts. They'd start a string (generally six or seven colts), ride them a few months, and turn the colts over to the cowboys. The twisters would then start another fresh string. Their methods were crude, often rough, but such training made for a good yardstick to measure the intelligence of a horse.

A colt would be run into a small round breaking pen. He'd generally be fore-footed and thrown. Sometimes he'd be caught by the neck and choked down. A hackamore with *fiador* would be slipped over his head and securely tied in place. The bronc rider would then mount a gentle horse and "lead" the bronc to a certain place to stake him out. He'd be tied to a log with a soft rope about thirty feet long and left to "eddicate" himself. The log was light enough to have a little give to it. When the bronc ran on the rope, he'd throw himself over and over again. He'd get tangled in the rope, fall, and rope-burn himself. The bronc rider would patiently untangle the colt and grease the rope burns. After a couple days of this, the colt wouldn't run on a rope and was hard to tangle up. Though rough, this was (and is) first-class horse breaking. Almost all the colts would permanently remember not to run on that rope and not to get tangled up in a rope. They'd never forget their lesson.

When the colt had learned his stake-out lesson and had healed up, he was brought to the breaking corral for the next step. His forelegs were looped with a soft rope, a blindfold was slipped over his wide-open eyes, and soft leather hobbles secured his front legs. A hind leg was drawn up and tied with another soft rope, the Scotch hobble. The blindfold was removed, and the colt was ready to be "sacked out."

Sacking out a colt simply means rubbing him all over with an old gunny sack, then flipping it over the colt until he's accustomed to a flipping, darting object being brushed all over him. It was and is a fine method to gentle a horse. A lesson a day for a few days generally made the bronc fairly gentle to be around. And it made saddling much easier.

When the colt accepted the waving sack, the saddle could be brought up with it. Before long the rig was eased down on the quivering back and lightly cinched up. Saddle in place,

Tangled in the rope.

Sketch by Dave Jones

the Scotch hobble was removed, freeing the hind hoof. A rope was tied to the hobbles in case the colt wanted to run or buck with the empty saddle. If the colt did "explode," he was jerked off his feet to "lay awhile." When allowed to regain his feet, he would never again try to escape the saddle. When the saddle could be put on and removed with no more than hobble restraint, the colt was ready to ride.

With hackamore reins tied on the *bosal* (noseband) instead of the stake and lead rope, saddle in place and cinched down, the rider removed the hobbles and stepped up. The starry-eyed colt stood there, back humped up, ready to "blow the plug." And almost all of them did.

When Mr. Bronc Twister moved the colt, the bronc's first action was to drop his head, let out a roar, and try to shed a cowboy. This was natural; all colts did it, and the twisters didn't like one that didn't. When the rider stayed and rode, bucking soon diminished to crowhops and ended up with a run around the pen. The colt breaker wanted to start, stop, turn both ways, and get on and off a few times. This constituted a good first ride (and it still does).

When the rider thought the colt had had enough, he'd reach forward and slip a browband blindfold down over the colt's eyes or interfere with vision by cupping his hand around the eyes. If the colt showed good sense through all this and the rider stayed on top, the rider was very pleased with the colt and praised him to all who'd listen. There's much personal satisfaction in such work.

From this point on it was just plain horse training. The colt would be ridden a few days in the small corral and then graduated to a larger pen, where he'd learn to lope in circles, start and stop, and to turn this way and that. The rider would accustom the colt to a swinging lariat. He'd catch a light log and drag it around the pen. After a couple of weeks of this, he'd give the colt some air by riding him outside on the open range. If the rider was a lucky one, he'd have a buddy who'd go along on a gentle horse.

When the months passed and the colts were gentle, they were driven to the remuda and distributed to the cowboys. The bronc twister generally had some suggestions about which cowboys should get which horses. A good old cowboy who could bring out the best in a colt would be favored by getting the twister's brightest pupils.

At any rate, all the colts had a chance to show their brains and willingness. If they learned, they made cow horses and always had the easiest work and the shortest rides. A cow horse would often be led to the herd, then ridden to separate marketable steers, calves to be weaned, and so on. The horse that didn't have the brains would be used to circle or gather.

A circle, or gather, horse was one with no great intelligence or training that was used to gather cattle. On an outside circle the horse might have to go all day. Old spoiled semioutlaws, the brutes of the cow-horse world, could be used for this.

Some cow outfits could say with pride that all their horses were ridden. Rough, fast horse breaking produced some rank horses, and "bronc stompers" were hired to ride these broncs at special pay. The men wanted only rough horses in their string, for they took pride in being top riders. They knew very little about horse training, but they did know how to ride bad horses. These riders were a different breed from the twisters who started the colts. Rough string riders became the rodeo bronc riders of yesterday and today.

I don't think a better system has ever been devised to separate intelligent horses from stupid horses than the training method used by the bronc twisters. All the horses had the same chance to be cow horses, and many made it. Some didn't. Today a horse owner will bring his colt to a trainer and say, "I want this colt to be a cutting horse." The trainer must take *this* colt and make him cut cattle if he wants his pay. Old ways were good. The natural cow horse showed his cow sense, and the stupid horse was culled.

The degree of intelligence in horses varies greatly. When a psychologist says that a horse has less intelligence than an elk, he doesn't take this into consideration. The psychologist would do well to handle horses for awhile.

A lifetime of experience with horses will make anyone wonder about the intelligence of a horse. I'll never forget Curley. Curley was a horse I knew at the Wildcat Ranch, in the Wildcat Hills, near Gering, Nebraska. Many years ago I was employed by this ranch as a horse breaker. It was a dude ranch, but Curley wasn't an ordinary dude horse.

Curley was one rugged individual. When feeding, he continually lashed out with his hind hoofs to keep his equine associates at their distance. He was old, small, and crippled with ringbone. His vicious display of bad manners ensured ample meals, for his unrelenting kicking was too much for even the crankiest mare.

Curley was tough to corral and ride. Most horses join their companions (herd instinct) when being corralled and meekly trail into the pen, even though by doing so they'll be caught and forced to work. Not so with Curley. He'd slip away at the first opportunity, and the unfortunate wrangler would have a hard, fast ride getting that shaggy pony into the corral. I once tore a fingernail off racing through the brush trying to point Curley toward home.

I'd ridden Curley, and he was pure bronc, ready to kick me or buck me off. Since he was crippled and little, I rode him only a couple of times, just to try him. I couldn't figure out why he was so mean with me. I guess he thought I was a rider and he could vent his spleen on me.

There was a dude who always rode Curley, and this, to me, was almost beyond belief. This man had been crippled with polio as a child. He walked with two canes or crutches. Curley was his reason for coming to the ranch. The little, rough-looking black horse was a very smooth ride, not at all like the ordinary run of dude horses. There was more that made the man think so highly of the horse.

I couldn't imagine how that crippled man could get on and stay on such a bronc when I was asked to bring him in for the man to ride. This is what I saw, time after time: The man propped his canes against the corral poles and, with help, climbed the fence until he was perched facing the horse, ready to mount. Then everyone backed away. Curley slowly sidled up to the man, looking around frequently to check his position. The man slowly and laboriously climbed from the fence to the waiting horse and pulled himself into position. This act would take a few minutes, during which time Curley never moved. No one held him. He did his best to help his crippled partner get aboard. When they moved out, Curley took care to move steadily and easily all day, balancing himself to help his unsure rider stay up. This procedure was well documented, for it was witnessed many times by the ranch owner, the help, and a flock of guests.

And then there's ol' Bullet, a horse I was hired to train not too many years ago at Leesburg, Virginia. Bullet was a nice fat three-year-old bay colt. He'd been ridden a little by the owner's kids. Three or four of them would hoist themselves on the colt. Bullet, like Curley, would never hurt anyone.

To give you an idea of this colt's brain power, during fly

Bullet

Sketch by Dave Jones

39

season Bullet would hunt up an old feed sack, get a good bite on it, and use it for a flyswatter.

I rode Bullet into a bunch of cattle on his first trip outside the corrals. He wanted to play with them and was ducking and dodging with a cow after ten minutes in the open pasture. He'd been ridden by me about a week. I told his owner that Bullet would make a cow horse.

So training went on. The colt liked playing with the cattle but was a little lazy. He'd sometimes allow a cow to slip by him because he hated to get out and really run. A bat (a mild training whip) wouldn't get enough speed out of him, so I decided to try spurs.

Spurs in place, I mounted ol' Bullet (even when he was a colt in training for two weeks, we called him ol' Bullet). He moped around the barnyard, and I touched him with the steel. Ol' Bullet let out a bellow and bucked me off.

Talk about bucking! I lost his head and my seat the first jump. My timing lost (never found), the third jump found me flying way above Bullet at the end of my hackamore reins. As they say in the song "Strawberry Roan," "I turned over twice an' come back down to earth." On the way down I met Bullet as he was coming up, which flipped me over again to make me land on my back with enough force to bury one of my spurs in dried-out clay.

"As I lay there, sprawling all over the ground" ("Strawberry Roan" again), I managed to look, between groans, for Bullet. He was still bucking and bellowing but soon looked around in amazement when he saw me on the ground. This curious sight stopped his pitching, and he trotted up to look me over.

As soon as I could get straightened out to remount Bullet, we ambled out to the breaking pen, where I easily educated him to spurs. He was never any more trouble.

40

Bullet never was a contest cutting horse, but he was a top ranch cow horse. I roped a lot of calves on him for branding and dehorning. We doctored many a cow together. He showed me his cow sense when he was still a green colt.

Charley, Bullet's owner, stopped at the barn one day and said that we had a little cow penning to do. Since it wouldn't be a hard ride, we loaded Bullet. Some ranch work would do him good.

But he had to work too hard. The penning seemed to be generally fouled up. The other horses weren't working well. A cow would break from the bunch, and Bullet and I always had to bring her back. When the cows were finally corralled, the colt was too tired to roll. He stood, legs spraddled, breathing hard, trying to recover. After a while he looked better. He picked a shady spot in his pen and lay down for a snooze.

The cattle were run through a long wing, then up into a ramp to enter the truck. Men on foot did this, and the loading went smooth enough. But a half-dozen wild ol' cows decided they'd been pushed enough. Charging back to the pens, they scattered men like tenpins. Try as they would, the men couldn't get the last cows loaded.

I saw that there was no other recourse than to use Bullet. Waking him up, I saddled the played-out colt for his final work.

The cows moved easily away from us toward the wings of the ramp. But twenty feet from the truck they turned to charge back.

I spurred Bullet hard to wake him up, and he met the cows. Biting and striking, he blocked the cows with such ferocity that they were glad enough to load into the van. He even jumped backward and practically sat on one that tried the sneaky way to get past him. So, cows loaded, Bullet, with

41

a mouthful of cow hair, watched the truck depart. Tired as he was, he was all cow horse when the job was before him.

Another horse in my string was a four-year-old stud. He impressed me with his stupidity as much as Bullet impressed me with his brains. I even forget his name (a fancy one), so, for a paragraph or so, let's call him Fred.

Fred stumbled for no apparent reason. He'd fall flat on a smooth dirt road. When asked to stop and turn, Herculean effort on the part of the rider was required. Then he'd turn on the wrong end. But he could work. When fresh out of the stall, he'd work like a top one for about five minutes. After that he was nothing.

Cutting cattle was impossible for this horse. He'd quit and run off before he had time to learn anything. We decided to make a rope horse out of him.

I'd just started riding for this outfit and we had few facilities. The pen in which we kept roping and cutting cattle was bare of chutes or holding pens. When I wanted to rope, I'd have to lay in behind the bunch and pick the one I wanted. This was fine when starting a colt on rope work, but chutes were needed later on.

But, since there was no use teaching Fred anything, I affixed draw reins on a snaffle bit and roped some calves. This horse almost couldn't be stopped. I'd catch a calf, and Fred would follow it about five laps around the pen with me hauling on those draw reins with all my might. It was like pulling on a log. Every calf, every day, was the same. The horse learned nothing, so I decided to resort to more drastic methods.

We kept a two-year-old Brangus heifer with the roping calves, though I never roped her. I decided that she might teach this stud something.

Once in a while, with dumb horses, science fails, and we

go back to rough-and-tumble training methods. My plan was to tie on hard and fast, rope the heifer, step off, and let her educate the horse. The neck rope was tied high up by his jaw so she could really jerk him.

All went well up to a point. I ran Fred up behind the calves which were running wide open. I looped the heifer, and then things went wrong. When the heifer felt the rope jerk up on her neck, she veered hard to the right while the calves ran straight. Fred elected to follow the calves and I couldn't turn him.

Then I flew! I sailed on and on and on! I met the ground gradually, to roll a country mile, finally stopping when I rolled into the fence.

Discovering I wasn't hurt, I got right up and looked around for the wreckage. What a mess! The stud and the heifer were lying a rope's length apart. Once in awhile Fred would flick an ear. I walked over to the heifer and jerked the rope off her. She rolled her eyes, moaned a little, got up, and staggered off. Fred followed the same procedure and was soon up shaking the dirt off. This was one rough way to train a horse.

I wanted to see if Fred had learned his lesson, so I mounted up and headed for another calf. The horse ran right out like a good one, and I popped a loop on a calf. Fred stopped so hard he threw me twenty-five feet, right on top of the calf!

Chutes were made, and more horses were trained. I kept roping off Fred, but progress was very slow. After roping a couple of calves, he'd be just as crazy on Tuesday as he was on Monday.

Fred's owner stopped by to check the horse's training. I mounted, rode into the box, turned a calf out, caught it, and made my tie. It looked like Cheyenne. The owner was wildly enthusiastic. He wanted to rope a calf!

He mounted Fred, rode into the box, nodded for his calf, and out they came. Only the horse didn't rate the calf. He stampeded across the arena, hit the gate head-on and was halfway to town before his owner got him stopped. That ended Fred's career as a rope horse.

So scientists tell us that a horse's intelligence can be rated. It doesn't seem so to me. I could go on and on talking about "equine Einsteins" and could also talk about horses so stupid it's a wonder they can find the water bucket. They seem a lot like people. You'll find smart ones and dumb ones. An intelligent horse is a pleasure to ride and own. I don't want the other kind.

VII *Horsemanship*

Some people are horsemen and horsewomen; some aren't.
A man can ride horses all of his life and still not be a horseman. There seems to be a common bond, a sympathetic feeling, between some people and horses. The ones who don't
have this bond would do well to have another hobby or
vocation.

A horseman likes horses. He has a feeling for a horse and
doesn't abuse his equine friends unnecessarily.

How many times have you seen this? A big-hatted, booted
guy, maybe a horse owner, pays a visit to look at your horses.
He opens one stall after another but isn't satisfied with a
glance. He must have the whole picture. The only way he
can see the horse is to move it to the back of the stall, so he
slaps the horse full in the face. I used to grit my teeth at this
and put up with it—but no more. I say, "If you want to
look at this horse, I'll be happy to get a halter and lead him
out so you can see him better." I go in the stall first and stand
protectively at the horse's head.

I don't know who started the slap-the-horse-in-the-face
fad, but it's done so often some people must think it's smart.
Boy, it's enough of a chore getting a colt friendly enough to
walk up to you without some clown slapping him around.
Horsemanship is using your head. I'd as soon walk up to a
stranger and punch him in the belly as I would slap a horse
in the face.

Horses do some mighty dumb things, and anyone who handles them much is bound to lose his temper. I've handled horses all my life and am just beginning to be able to control mine. *Horsemanship is controlling your temper.*

How can you learn to control your temper? Answer: There are many horses you can't lose your temper with. These horses will stomp you if you do. When your temper is ready to boil over, picture a horse that will strike you quicker than a rattlesnake or tear your head off quicker than a lion. Will you boil over at such a horse? Heck no, he'd kill you! So it's not uncontrollable temper; it's human meanness coming to the front. It's a horse you can lose your temper with that you whip unmercifully. This temper can be controlled. It's horsemanship to do so.

I remember hearing cowboy tales about youngsters with bad temper habits. The old cowmen wouldn't put up with them. A young man who was too free with his spurs would have his horses switched, and he'd end up with a string of man-eaters. The foreman would say, "All right, young feller, let's see you put spur marks on them horses." This was good education, the kind a guy will remember.

Once, when more or less a kid, I worked for the Hatchet Cattle Company. My boss was J. L. Draper, of Wetmore, Colorado, one of the finest men I ever knew. Draper once wrote to me, a few years after I worked for him, that I had a job with him any time I wanted it and that he'd send transportation money if it was needed. I had never met a ranch manager with so much consideration for his riders. He once made a hard day's ride in my place because I had a little cough. He thought I might be catching something and wanted me to take it easy.

My string of horses consisted of ten horses, half of which were fairly gentle. These horses needed to be tough. They

46

were generally ridden hard all day because it was often impossible to get in at noon to change to a fresh mount. Worse, Draper had owned a string of bareback and saddle broncs. When a bronc quit bucking reliably, he was handled a little and put in the remuda if he was the correct type to make a saddle horse. But a horse has a long memory and often fondly remembers other days. Some of those horses had put down cowboys after being ridden thirty miles.

I hired on at the start of roundup. Art Williams, a great old cowboy, was the one who hired me and was my companion through roundup. He and I would gather about two thousand bovines, a pasture at a time, drive them to holding pastures close to camp, awaiting the day when cowboys from the home ranch would join us to start the five-day drive to the winter pastures. Our line camp was near Cripple Creek, Colorado.

A typical day started with me trying to find my wrangle horse in a small pasture. This was difficult because it was pitch dark. Catching him with some feed, I'd lead him to the bronc corral, hobble him, tie up a back foot, saddle and bridle him, and then remove the foot ropes. Since it was very cold in the morning in the high country, this little no-account horse always tried to buck me off. After our morning rodeo I'd ride out to find the horse herd and corral them while Art was busy cooking breakfast.

After eating breakfast and cleaning up the cabin, we'd go out to catch our horses for the day's ride. It was daylight by then, and I felt pretty good, or three men couldn't have gotten me on some of those horses. I'm a confirmed coward before breakfast.

Very few of the horses could be saddled unless we tied up a hind foot—a matter of course. Since we were riding so hard, a couple of doubled Navaho blankets were used to pad the saddle. And that saddle was impossible to get cinched on tight enough because the horse would inhale all the air he could hold and tense every muscle to the locking point. When the foot ropes were removed, it was easy to see that the next thing to do would be to *ride*.

Art always started out too fast. He'd lope out of camp after his mount quit pitching. I wanted to walk and trot until my horse moved freely. Art was wiser. He wanted our horses to get the rankness out close to camp rather than ten miles away, high in the mountains.

We'd hunt cattle until we had to start back. When day was done, the horses would be so tired that there was no meanness in them. So, if we had any daylight, we'd shoe the horses that seemed to wear out a new shoe in a couple of rides. We ate after the day's work and soon went to bed— morning came early. My appetite was spoiled thinking about the horse I had to ride the next day.

No matter how rough our horses were, we never kicked or hit one of them. I never saw a man considered to be a good cowboy whip a horse. Of course, cowboys carry bats or quirts with which to 'spank' a horse, but that isn't the same thing as the foolishness we see all the time now.

I often see so-called trainers hit their horses in the face with their rein ends for no reason at all. What would happen if you hit a rope horse in the eye like that? Why, when you roped, your horse would duck away from your arm and get you jerked down—or worse.

Remember: horsemanship is common sense and the built-in ability to get along with horses. It's knowing how a colt feels and figuring out why he does what he does. It's patience. It's knowledge and experience.

A horseman doesn't show off. A guy who'd run his horse up and down, spurring wildly, showing off, used to be known as a drug-store cowboy, though I haven't heard the term for a long time. A kid who'd run his horse back and forth, over-working him and agitating the cattle unnecessarily, was known as a "heel-fly" on the cow outfits. He would always be in the wrong place at the wrong time. He wouldn't last long unless he changed his ways. A string of rough horses gen-erally corrected this condition.

It's hard for a would-be horseman to get experience today unless he's around to observe a top hand. If you know a top hand who fits my description, do what he does, take his ad-vice, and you won't go wrong. But if you go in a trainer's barn and notice that his horses tremble in his presence, if he appears to hate horses by his attitude, avoid him like poison, because that's what he is—poison to horses.

VIII *Handling the Preriding-Age Colt*

I think you should handle, pet, and hand-feed a young colt often enough to gentle him and make friends with him. A colt that is your friend isn't as likely to hurt you as a colt that is your enemy.

There are all sorts of horses, so there are all sorts of colts. I used to manage a big horse ranch where the horses raised were Colombian Pasos. These aren't the kinds of horses that'll climb all over you if you're kind to them, but they respond in kind. Be affectionate with a Paso, and he'll return your favors. Get rough, and he'll dish out all the fight you want.

For example, while I was at this ranch, I got proud of my little cutting mare, Yocunda. She was doing a good job of cutting cattle, and I wanted her to look better. Her ears were bushy, so I decided to trim them with small animal clippers. I put a twitch (a loop or noose) on her nose, started the clippers, and reached for her ear. A front hoof lightly slapped me on each shoulder as a warning. She didn't try to hurt me, but I'd had my warning.

"Ol' honey, if you want your ears full of hair, it's O.K. with me," says I, removing the twitch and petting her on the neck. I appreciated her aim; my face was still intact.

Paso colts handle and gentle all right, but different methods from the ones I'd always used were called for. We discovered that colts weren't gentling quickly enough with the old proven methods, so we had to experiment with new methods.

Tying up a hind hoof, hobbling the front hoofs, rubbing and petting a colt, then rubbing and flopping a feed sack all over the colt had always proved successful. When the baby calmly accepted the waving sack, he was on his way to becoming gentle. Not so with the Pasos. A fairly gentle Paso colt would be made wild and afraid with such treatment.

We soon found that the blindfold was our greatest training aid. This, plus petting, grooming, and feeding tidbits from the hand, became correct Paso procedure.

Another time we noticed five colts and fillies, seven to eleven months old, that had to have their hoofs trimmed. They'd had no previous handling because we were always so busy that we let the youngsters get older before handling them much.

We had a small chute that was a wonderful aid when working with colts. It sure beat roping them. We drove a colt in the chute, shut the gate, blindfolded the colt, worked a halter on, and led the colt, *with the blindfold still on*, to the snubbing post. Hoofs could then be handled and trimmed with the colt offering little or no resistance.

If a colt fought, fell over backward, or got wedged in the chute, the whole side opened up, and he was released, no worse for the experience. The chute was padded with old truck-tire inner tubes. It was low enough that shots could be given in the neck of the animals. We depended on the blindfold to keep the colts on the ground. Without this they would have climbed the chute and gotten out. Even our vet was dubious about this low chute until he saw it work. We could give sleeping-sickness and tetanus shots to forty yearlings in less than two hours by using the chute.

I'd never cared much for the blindfold before then. I preach, in this book and my previous one, *Practical Western Training*, to stay flexible and accept new methods—to fit the

51

methods to the horse. So, here I am, after training for twenty-five years, using a tool that I'd never before liked.

I'd tried to blindfold colts before on a few occasions and had found it to be a poor business. Many colts became panic-stricken and threw themselves in a suicidal manner. You almost never see a blindfold used in this country. But, the blindfold is in general use in South America. In Peru it's part of the gear on the hackamores and bridles, called *tapaojos*. I saw it used time and again in Colombia, where people need to use every horse and mule. Almost all the mules are blindfolded when being packed.

I don't believe I would have thought of using the blindfold if I hadn't seen it so widely used in South America. We soon were blindfolding mares for shots, hoof trimming, doctoring, and the like and almost completely discarded the twitch.

One time we had a filly to doctor. She was a four-year-old with a hormone imbalance. I took a twitch with me, roped the filly, and screwed the twitch on her nose. Then the vet brought the shot. Popping the needle in her vein produced quick results. She reared and struck, hitting me in the shoulder before I could blink.

Now, you don't fight these Pasos. You try to get along with them, as you should with any horse. I knew that I might have to throw her and tie her down, but I tried the blindfold first. She stood, never moving at all, had her shot, and was released with no trouble.

From all this I found the blindfold to be a very useful tool in horse handling. Nothing could be simpler to make. Cut a slit for the ears in a thirty-by-thirty-inch cheap cotton saddle blanket. A hole to tie a string in and another hole opposite can secure the blindfold under the jaw.

If you want a blindfold on your hackamore, soft latigo

How to restrain a bronc. Ken Serco flips a blindfold on the bronc as Bill Coleman holds the lead rope.

Here's a look at the blindfold we favor. Strings attached to it let us tie it under the bronc's jaw.

A colt is driven into the pen that leads to the chute.

makes a good one. It's rigged right under the browband, on the headstall. The slits should be small so it will stay in place until you want to pull it down.

We didn't always get to handle colts as much as we should, but, "Do as I say, not as I do." Let's talk about how a young horse should be handled.

When a colt is weaned, he'll be lonesome and sick, wanting his mother. It's much better if he has company. The best company is another colt, or colts, for misery loves company.

I wouldn't handle the colt much until he gets over the weaning and forgets Mama. You can't teach him anything until he's over his grief. These colts love their mothers a lot, and you should respect this. When he seems interested in food and has quit yelling for his mother, you can start handling him.

The colt is trapped in the chute. If wild, a blindfold is applied first, then the colt is haltered. A rope is tied around his neck with a bowline knot and passed through the halter. There is less chance for the colt to break or kink his neck if the rope is back eight inches from where the pull of the halter would be.

The first thing is to halter the colt. If you've been smart and have had the time, you already have him gentle, easy to halter, and broken to lead. If you've been really smart, you did this when the colt was still on his mother.

This advice is for beginners or for busy ones—for those whose colt is weaned but has never been caught before.

You should have some help. You need to have the colt in a safe enclosure to catch him. A box stall is fine. Try to pet the colt or scratch him where he itches. If he'll stand for this, he may get so interested that haltering him is a cinch. If not, one man can grab the colt by the neck while another grabs the tail and pushes it straight up, tight, over the colt's back. This will immobilize him so haltering can be accom-

The chute is yanked open. The trainer with the long lead rope will try to get the colt to the snubbing post.

plished. With the tail still held up, the colt can be scratched and petted for gentling. When the tail is released, the colt will jump, rear, and probably fall over backwards.

A good way to keep a colt down on the ground is to tie a soft rope around the girth, run the rope between the fore-legs and through the halter. Seldom will a colt rear over back-wards with such a rig. I favor the nonslip bowline knot for this.

The next step is to lead and tie up the colt. You can man-handle him safely with the rope through the halter. All this should be performed as calmly as possible.

We had a range cube formulated for horses. The cubes are high in protein and the horses love them. I find them to be a great aid when colt-gentling. There has always been discus-sion and argument about feeding horses tidbits from the

The first step in getting a colt to the snubbing post. Bill Coleman has pulled the colt around and is working his way to the post.

hand. The rough-and-tough cowboy wants none of this. I remember Will James writing about sugar-fed pets—spelled "pests"—that they were all over you for a handout. He didn't like it, and a great many people agree with him.

I must be truthful about it because it sure-enough makes some horses pests. When I take people out to see the brood herd, several mares will pester a person until his nerves are raw. But it's nice to be able to catch the horse you want without corralling the whole bunch. It's nicer to have friendly horses than try to show horses that are scared to death of a man.

Today, at my own stables, we use these cubes when gentling colts. The young fellows have learned to eat them while still nursing Mama and will take them from the hand as soon as they understand that the human is to be trusted.

The colt is snubbed and is pulling back. The position of the rope, pulling back at least eight inches behind the ears, is a safety factor for the colt.

Rings set in a solid wall make good articles to tie colts to, for the system is almost foolproof. There's nothing for the colt to get caught in. When he learns that getting away is impossible and that fighting the rope is foolish, we step in with some cubes so that he won't hate being handled so much. We also pet him and scratch his itchy places. His hoofs are handled and trimmed. If we have a colt that's bad about all this, we blindfold him. If a colt fights and doesn't gentle quickly, we take him to the snubbing post in the bronc corral, because it's a bit dangerous to work a broncy colt that's tied to a solid wall—there's not enough room for the person to get away safely.

Tying up colts is often enough to break them to lead. They learn that running back on the rope won't work. Some need

There is no give in a snubbing post. Most colts realize this and stop fighting very quickly.

more treatment, and we use the standard loop around the rump for this. We'll walk around the arena with the colt, stopping now and then to give him a few range cubes. After an hour of this most colts lead fairly well. If a colt leads, is fairly gentle, and will allow us to trim his hoofs, I consider this enough. He should be handled enough to stay gentle.

One word of caution. I've talked a lot about using range cubes as a gentling aid. Remember that we've had these made especially for horses. The regular range cube for cattle contains urea, which isn't good for horses and can even poison them. There is a cube made for cattle without urea that is perfectly safe for horses.

Tied to a snubbing post, this colt is rubbed and petted by Ken Serco to get him used to humans.

I don't care to drive or longe a young colt because he can be temperamental and made cranky with too much handling. I think that the average colt should be kept gentle, leading, and friendly. He's better off out in the pasture, growing up normally, than in a stall being handled all the time.

With the colt tied to a snubbing post, it's a good time to handle his legs and hoofs.

This colt leads fairly well after his short session at the snubbing post.

IX *Training a Colt*

Starting the colt on his way to lifelong work as a saddle horse needs to be done correctly. A good start is vitally important in the making of a good horse.

The previous chapter brings us up to the time when the colt is ready for training. This chapter covers the initiation to the saddle and the first month that he is ridden. I assume that the colt will lead, is fairly gentle, and will allow the trainer to handle his hoofs.

Many trainers advocate use of the longe line at this time. In a way it's good, and in a way it's bad. The colt needs to learn to walk, trot, and canter in small circles. This is called suppling. You can teach the colt to start, stop, and work on voice command on the longe line. This is all very good if one has the time for it. It's great if you have only one or two colts to train.

The aspect of the longe line that I don't like is that you may *always* have to precede your ride with a longe-line session if the animal becomes accustomed to it. I like to be able to take a colt (or horse) right out of a stall, saddle up, and go. A lot depends on the individual horse. I think longeing a colt is fine if it isn't overdone.

My next step is getting the colt used to saddling. The prelude to this is sacking the colt out. The colt may be tied to a post or a ring on the wall or may be hobbled. I prefer hobbles, for hobble training is very valuable. The colt learns to

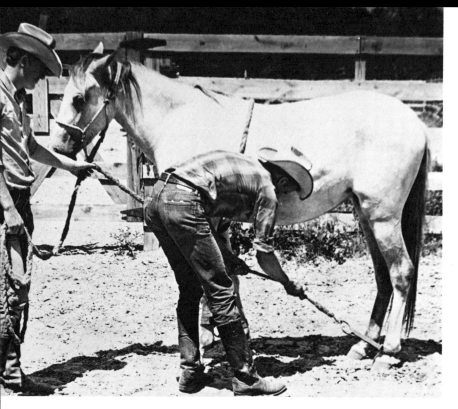

Jeff Lacy, an apprentice trainer, holds a horse while Ken Serco applies the side-line.

stand on hobbles, a method which often makes doctoring, saddling, and so on, much easier. Since I hate to see a horse "ground-tied," pasture hobbles are good for future camping and cookouts. Most colts respond to sacking much better hobbled than they do when just tied to a post.

First, a hind leg is hobbled—that is, pulled up high enough to hinder mobility but not so high as to make it impossible for the colt to put any weight on it. There will be a little fighting about this so-called Scotch hobble, but a colt already broken to lead won't fight much. When he stands quietly and isn't too excited to eat a range cube, the front legs are hobbled. This hobble is made of soft latigo leather. I prefer buckling it around the pasterns, right above the hoofs, rather than

The hobbles and side-line in place.

higher up around the cannon bone. There's less chance of injury to the colt if he should fight the hobbles. This type of hobble is often called the Utah hobble.

If the colt fights much, he may fall, so it's best to work in a corral deep with sand or soft earth. Sometimes he's unable to regain his feet when hobbled. If this is the case, the Scotch hobble should be removed and the colt allowed to get up. The hind leg may then be tied up again. Before long the colt will cease fighting and stand up like a good one. Some petting and a range cube go well when this happens.

Finally, the sack is brought into the picture. I rub the colt all over with it. When he stands for the rubbing, I start to rub faster. Finally, I flip the sack all over the colt, taking care never to slap him in the face or cause him any pain. When he stands for this, he can be saddled easily.

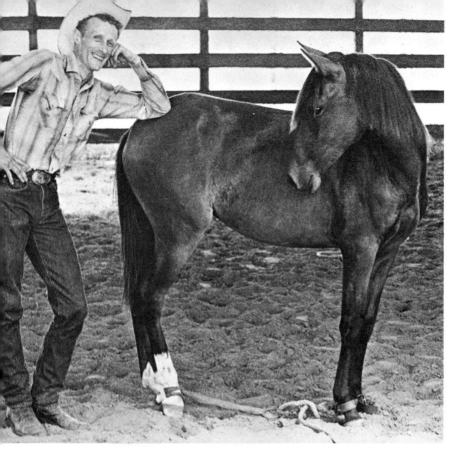

Ken Serco demonstrates the effectiveness of hobbles and the side-line to restrain this yearling filly.

But, as I said before, some colts get wild during the sacking. Many Pasos can't stand it, and the trainer would be foolish to continue such a course. This nervy-type colt needs to gain confidence in his trainer. We find that a thorough grooming will work perfectly with such a colt. The grooming feels good, and the colt soon stands for the curry comb, brush, and tail comb. We hobble all colts during this stage of their training.

Whether gentled by sacking or by grooming, the colt finds

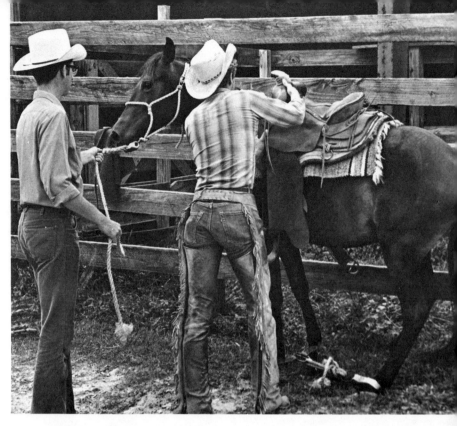

With the hobbles and the side-line still in place, the blindfold is removed and the bronc is saddled.

little to object to about the saddle. A little flurry should be expected when the cinch is drawn up. Never throw a saddle on any horse—even the gentlest will soon become unmanageable if the stirrup whacks him on his elbow often enough. If the colt bucks or tries to buck, he'll be hampered enough by his hobbles to make a poor job of it. Never lose your temper with a colt. If he fights, you're hurrying too much.

When the colt is saddled, the hobbles should be removed. All clear, the colt should be led around for a short time. Make much of him. Tell him he's a good horse, and give him some cubes. Unsaddling should be easy if the front feet are hob-

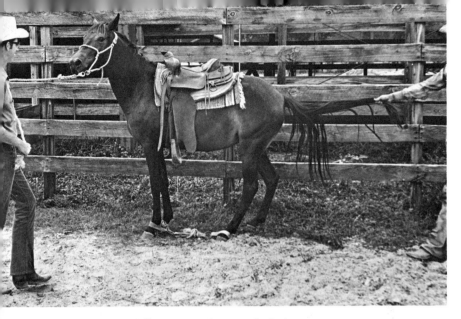
Efforts are made to gentle the bronc.

bled. The next time he's saddled, the front (Utah) hobbles should be enough.

The next day longeing may be started. For this, we like the California hackamore, the reins tied up to prevent bucking. The longe line is attached anywhere on the back of the hackamore. Start the colt in circles around you and gradually feed him line until he's working out where you want him. This is all pretty easy stuff. Go on with longeing as long as you care to. I find no fault with it. But *for me*, I want to go on with the next step as soon as possible. The colt is learning things in an orderly fashion, so I don't want to get hung up on one thing early in his training. He thinks new things will happen to him regularly, so if we don't proceed, the next step can become harder.

I am an avid fan of Henry Wynmalen. His books *Equitation* and *Dressage* should be in every horseman's library. But his next step would be to ride the colt, and here is where Wynmalen and I disagree. I think a bit of driving in longe

Ponying the bronc before the ride.

lines helps any colt as long as the trainer knows what he's about. Wynmalen prefers to do everything beyond longeing from the colt's back. I think the initial training is speeded up, with less wear and tear on the colt, if he learns a few things in driving lines.

For instance, the colt immediately learns to turn, start, and stop. A great benefit of longe-line driving is that the colt can easily and safely be backed, and he will retain this knowledge. So we drive most of them.

I'm quite sure Wynmalen isn't acquainted with the hackamore. I don't like to drive colts in a snaffle bit. The hackamore is an ideal tool for this purpose. Longe lines are affixed to the hackamore (braided rawhide—not the stupid metal hackamore), stirrups are hobbled (tied beneath the colt's belly), longe lines are run through the stirrups, and we're ready to go.

Driving the colt is best accomplished if it's carried out in a small training pen. We have one forty by forty feet that's

Ride 'em! Bill Coleman wishes he'd left the hobbles on the bronc.

ideal. The colt can't, in such a small area, get away from his trainer. The trainer can soon stand still in the center of the pen and drive the colt around him. If your pen is larger, a helper would be handy. He could lead the colt until the trainer feels secure in his control over the colt.

There is almost always a flurry when the driving line first rubs against the colt's buttocks. This can't be avoided. This flurry is of short duration, and the colt is soon being driven in fine fashion.

71

Ken Serco drives a colt in longe lines.

Letting the colt circle the pen for five or ten minutes gives him time to get used to the unusual. Then he can be easily stopped by heading him into the fence and holding him there. "Whoa" should be clearly spoken when the colt is asked to stop. In a few more minutes the colt can easily be stopped away from the fence. Generally the colt can be asked to back and he will do so. A few steps should be asked for. Backing shouldn't be overdone this first time in longe lines.

Many colts respond so well to the driving procedure that I give them their first ride right after the drive. As I said, I like to keep new things coming at them until they're ridden. I've done this so many times that I know whether or not the colt will give me a good first ride. The person new to training should take more time. A week or two of driving in the longe lines won't hurt a thing. The colt should start and stop in fine fashion by then, perhaps almost working by vocal signals alone. He should back readily, straight, and fast. With no weight on his back to hinder him, with a very low pull on the reins, he should work better in longe lines than he will in the near future when carrying a rider. The low pull and all the leverage the trainer has at his command, if needed, force the colt into correct work.

Care should be taken not to misuse the leverage. Longe lines should be handled very lightly, with intermittent pulls and releases—never a steady hard pull. Even in longe lines a colt will fight a steady pull on the hackamore.

When the colt works lightly and calmly in longe lines, the next step is getting on and riding. You will be amazed by the ease of the first ride after the colt has had correct initial training.

During longe-line training I often walk up to the colt, stick a toe in the stirrup, and ease up (but never clear up) on him. I wouldn't ride in longe lines, so this is insurance that I won't get on him. The temptation to do so is often very strong. In this way he becomes accustomed to a little weight and seeing me stand up on him. If he does anything but stand, I step right down to try it later. Before I ride, the colt will stand perfectly still for mounting.

The day comes for the first ride! The colt handles well in longe lines so there's no point in continuing such training. The hobbles come off, and the hackamore is rigged for riding. The colt may appear a bit nervous because the trainer very possibly is a bit nervous and communicates this to the colt. This feeling will pass when the colt moves out and shows the trainer that he handles.

I think that anyone, no matter how many colts he's started, is a bit nervous about riding a colt for the first time. We all dread the unknown. We know that the colt will go in fine fashion, but still . . . . The colt does go fine. He jumps around a little when he feels the trainer on his back. The live weight of a rider is new to him. But the basic training has been thorough enough so that the colt starts, stops, and responds to the pull of the reins.

The rider uses his legs right from the start even though they mean next to nothing to the colt. The rider uses his left leg with intermittent pressure, on and off, for a right turn.

Hackamoring a colt is both a science and an art. If the propaganda I've heard about the hackamore is true, it dates back to early California. The word hackamore comes from the Spanish word *jáquima* (*hah-kee-mah*) and means "noseband." When Spaniards started the cow business in California, almost everything made of metal had to be shipped from Spain. A Spanish finishing bit, generally some form of spade, would last a horseman all of his life. Colt training bits were something else. They weren't worth enough to bother shipping. So the California hackamore was invented. The California horseman developed its use until it was a fine art. Top trainers jealously guard their secrets of *jáquima* training, passing them down, father to son, to this day.

I learned basic hackamore use from a great California trainer and then worked, year after year, perfecting its use. I'm better with the *jáquima* than with the snaffle bit, accomplishing more, quicker and better, than I would with a colt bit. Some trainers are better with the snaffle bit. I'm a hackamore man and train almost all the colts I work by the old California methods. Some colts have bad noses and good mouths. I snaffle-bit this kind because you can't make a hackamore horse if the horse just isn't suited for it.

The one great main truth about the hackamore is that you must *never use a steady pull*. It's always pull and release, pull and release. When a steady pull is used, the colt will, at

74

Dave Jones on Sugar Bow Girl, stopping in loose reins, in the early stages of training.

75

Ken Serco on Baron. A good hackamore colt can often be ridden with only a piece of rope around his neck.

Show-off stuff. This picture dramatically illustrates the sensitivity of a hackamore horse. Dave Jones up.

best, lean into the *jáquima* and get hard. He can "bull" into it (taking his head away from his rider to run away), buck, or do as he wants to. For every action there's a reaction. Pull steadily on the hackamore and the colt will pull steadily against you.

When a colt wants to run or buck, the rider's natural tendency is to pull hard and steadily. This reaction is the main thing to avoid because it will get you in trouble right away. Trying to stop a horse by means of a steady pull on the reins is like trying to lift yourself in the air by pulling your bootstraps.

If the colt starts running, the correct procedure is to take his head by getting a short hold on a rein and pulling suddenly and hard enough to turn the colt completely around. This is called the "double" and is the only correct hackamore control. The colt learns that he can be doubled. If he knows that his rider can double him anytime, no matter what resistance he puts up, he'll give in to a straight-back light pull, slow down, and stop when the rider wants him to.

Many of the rough-tough boys know little or nothing of true hackamore control. They wrap wire around the noseband and handle the colt with such brute force as to leave permanent scars on the nose. The horse trained in such fashion will never make a hackamore horse. Such gimmicks as metal hackamores have no place in the knowledgeable trainer's stable. They can only spoil colts and get you in trouble.

A small, high training pen is the place to keep a colt until control is a sure thing. It's much easier to turn a running colt into the fence with a double if the pen is small and the rider is confident. The situation is different in a large pasture, where even an expert may freeze on the reins.

Riding in the pen, the trainer should keep his hands very

low. When turning the colt with pulls and releases, the pulling hand should be a foot below the colt's withers. Too much pressure is exerted on the jaw if the hands are higher. High hands will make a colt throw his head because the pull has a twisting, grating effect on his jaw. Pull no higher than his head at normal carriage.

When pulling back to stop, always pull with one rein. *Pull and release*. If he doesn't stop, pull and release again. After a few more tries with no results, double the colt. Try again. No results? Double the other way. He'll soon respond if you reward him when he does stop.

The colt may get extremely excited when doubled. Or he may not associate the double with slowing and stopping. In that case the best policy is to work the colt in small circles until he calms down, gets tired of circling, and stops. It's best to get along with the colt without a fight. It's all new to him, and time will make the difference. The colt should double easily before the trainer makes any attempt to ride him out of the small breaking pen. You have no control until the colt understands the double.

Do *you* understand the double? Remember, when the colt misbehaves, you work the double from a slack rein. Take the rein about a foot and a half from the hackamore, pull quickly and with enough force to jerk the colt around in his track. A larger turn than this is too easy on the colt. This is punishment; the colt must dread it if it is to be effective. The rein hand should be held as low as possible. You *must* double from slack rein. You must turn the colt around abruptly in his own tracks. Don't confuse this with a rollback, in which the colt is jerked right around with no attempt at any kind of form. You are only teaching him to respond to hackamore signals.

A few years ago I was riding a big stout broncy filly in a

large pasture. She was too strong to be forced into anything. As we passed a little lake, a flock of Canadian geese stormed up into the air with enough racket to wake a hibernating bear. The filly jumped, ready to explode in a wild stampede. My move credited my many years as a trainer. When she was sailing twenty feet through the air, I flipped slack and threw a hard double on her. She lit circling and jumping. I doubled her again and again—every time she wanted to run. I could feel the thump of her heartbeat. Previous doubling in the training pen had taught her that she couldn't get away from me. She soon stood, legs spraddled, heart pounding, watching the spot where the honkers had been. I then let her trot around in small circles for a few minutes before walking her slowly to the barn.

I've read training books and articles that denounced the double as very crude stuff. One noted author bases his line of training on "trembling the hands." This is all fine, but the double has saved my skin a great many times. It's the basic ingredient in hackamore training because, if the colt has no respect for the hackamore, he's not a hackamore horse. Doubling from a slack rein is like a fat lady's diet. It's darn hard to stick to. Read and reread this part about the double. Make sure you understand it. You need to be capable of doubling a colt before attempting hackamore training. Remember, without the double, guys put wire on the noseband —which is *really* crude stuff. You never need to get a hackamore horse sore. His respect for the double will make him extremely light.

From all this emphasis on the double you might gather that a colt is doubled at every ride. This isn't the case. You double only when you need to. Too much doubling will make a colt nervous and limber-necked, which means he'll stick his head in your lap and go straight ahead instead of turning.

You may have to double a colt only once in his life. If he has enough respect, this could well be the case. Never double just to be doubling.

Let's see how doubling fits into the rest of training. When you want to slow down or stop, one rein is pulled straight back and released. If the colt shoots his nose up, you immediately bring it down with the other rein. This action could be compared with sawing on the bit. So, when stopping, one rein is pulled and the other is kept ready in case it's needed. Don't pull the second rein unless it's needed. If you want to turn the colt back into the fence, first pull the rein on the fence side, or the direction you want the colt to turn. Left turn, left rein. You also use leg aids. Get up off the saddle, squeeze with both legs to collect the horse to slow or stop. Leg aids are coupled with rein signals. So, left turn, left rein and right leg pressure. *Always use leg aids.* You are lazy if you don't use leg aids.

When all goes well, the colt will respond to your rein signals, the shift of your body weight, and your leg aids. You'll soon notice your colt shooting his hind legs up under him when he gets these signals. The rein signal to slow or stop is called the "tuck" because the hackamore colt should tuck his chin in, not throw his nose out and up. When you slow or stop, you tuck the colt. An additional aid is the voice. Say, "Whoa," when stopping and "E-e-e-e-easy," when slowing down. Your aids are (1) rein signals, (2) the shift of body weight forward and weight in the stirrups, (3) a squeeze and release with the legs, and (4) vocal signals. These four aids are applied to slow down and/or stop. If you get no immediate response to your signals, double the colt. Don't scream, rant, rave, hit, or kick the colt. Simply, calmly, double him. Keep your cool. Don't double with great force. Use just enough muscle to do the job.

81

Our next step is to start teaching the colt *how* to turn around. There are two methods. The first is the most popular method. This consists of getting a whip, bat, club, or chain and hammering on the colt's neck until he turns to get away from the fright and pain. The other method is an old California one.

Let's assume that you want to teach the colt to turn correctly. This means that he should roll over his hocks, turn on the haunches, or turn on the rear end. Understand? A club isn't actually needed. The colt is walked alongside the fence, stopped, allowed or forced to stand ("dwell"), then abruptly swung into the fence and jumped out into a run. He is jumped out by using leg pressure or a light tap with the training whip. You tap him on the rump; don't hit him on the neck or face. Keep the colt four or five feet from the fence so that he can easily turn into it without being forced to back or rear up. The dwell is very important.

If you don't stop before turning, you actually force the colt to turn on the forehand. A turn on the forehand is a dressage maneuver but has no use with the stock or reining horse. Picture the action in your mind. Go down the fence, stop, swing the colt quickly into the fence, and jump him out. Swinging him into the fence and jumping him out forces him to make a 180-degree turn, a turn from north to south. His hoofs are planted north. When he lands running, his hoofs face south with no in-between tracks. This is a correct half turn. It might take a couple of months to get the colt to the point where he automatically does a correct half turn away from the fence. Stay with it. Keep the jump-out if you want a correct turn because the speed makes it correct. Slow down, and the colt will learn to skip around. Remember to work both ways. If the colt works well to the left but is sloppy turning to the right, work him twice as much to the right.

Most trainers sincerely believe that a horse naturally works better on one side. I think that it's the trainer's fault. We people are right- or left-handed, and we practice most what's easiest for us. A right-handed person holds the reins in his left hand. He'll carry a bat in his right hand. It's easier for him to work the colt to the left, so most right-handed trainers make left-footed horses. The trainer must think of this and make a point of reining with his right hand a good portion of the time.

The rollback is something we seldom see executed correctly. The 180-degree turn is the basis of the rollback. The poor work we see is due to lack of the dwell. The dwell can be five minutes or a fraction of a second, but the dwell must be put into the rollback for a correct rollback over the hocks. Why?

Another name for the rollback is the set-and-turn. The dwell can be the fraction of a second when the horse's front hoofs hit the ground. If you turn him before the hoofs hit, he'll skid around, partly using his front end. Give him the split second necessary for his hoofs to hit, get set to swing his body around with his front legs, and he *can* execute a correct rollback. Spins, pivots, quarter turns and half turns are all related because in each case the horse is working over his hocks and because the dwell in the set-and-turn is a vital necessity to correct work.

Remember the "double," the "tuck," and the "dwell."

Circling is a very good exercise for the colt. He should get some of this with every ride. I like to lope the colt on a large circle and gradually draw it in until the circle is small. A sixty-foot circle drawn into a ten-foot circle is about right. I always circle both ways. When learning to circle, the colt will get a bit stiff and sore, so a little of this goes a long way at first. Gradually build him up. Circling will really muscle a colt, making him handy and supple. A supple colt can be bent into the circle and gives with his whole body.

The colt's head should turn *slightly into* the circle. Light low pulls and releases will soon have the colt turning into your hand with almost no rein pressure. For this reason the hand should come way out from the horse with each light pull. This is called a wide rein and should be used for a month. When the motion can be brought in a bit you're using a direct rein, not a wide rein. A direct rein is a straight pull on hackamore or bit. The indirect rein is the neckrein.

When circling to the left, intermittent pressure is applied with the right leg. Once in a while a colt will give too much to the leg and will move his rear in, which forces his head out away from the circle. The result is a circle that becomes small much too rapidly when you try to keep his head into the circle. In this case you must use left leg pressure to hold the back of the horse out. This will allow you to keep some size to the circles.

Work should go like this for a left circle. Lightly pull the colt's head to the left and use right leg pressure to get the correct left lead. When the colt swings his rear in, overly responding to leg pressure, quickly apply left-leg pressure to force the rear out. Light pulls on the hackamore will keep the head slightly in toward the direction of the circle.

The colt can pick up many bad habits in the arena. He gets bored with work or will overly respond—anticipating work and acting before he gets a signal. Then it's time to get the colt into a pasture.

Many meticulous horsemen always work in a pen. Their horses never know the pasture. This is especially true of dressage trainers. But these trainers, masters of their craft, are supersensitive to the horse's slightest fault and know how to correct it. Many dressage horses have nervous habits, such as tail wringing, that are impossible to correct.

A reining horse should be worked quite a bit in the pasture. He'll be interested in being out and won't overwork. Ten minutes circling in the arena, with an occasional roll-back, is enough. A leisurely ride in the pasture is fun. A little reining work in a grassy meadow is fine training. We had many miles of trails at Meridian Meadows, and I never saw a colt that didn't enjoy the trails. A little work in the pen plus a nice trail ride keeps a colt happy.

If trails are a bit hazardous, it's best to go with another rider on a gentle horse for a few times before soloing. But don't stick the colt behind the gentle horse because he'll soon get into the habit of following along like a pack horse. Keep the colt out in front or alongside the other horse.

Back a few paragraphs I mentioned tail wringing. This is a habit no one likes, and you'll see it in a great many Quarter Horses. It can be avoided.

People who own Quarter Horses like a short tail on a horse. This is often carried to a ridiculous point. A horse was meant to have both a mane and a tail or they wouldn't be growing there in the first place. I roach the mane on a rope horse if that's his sole use. Period. I like a neat tail on a horse but not an excessively short one.

A man buys a colt to break and immediately shortens his tail. The tail feels different to the colt. He's a little agitated with the training and starts wringing his tail. It's like a person who has had a tooth pulled—he can't keep his tongue away from the cavity in his mouth because it's something new.

A trainer brings in some colts to break from the back pasture. Their tails drag the ground. Before anything else, he pulls the tails. Then he starts breaking colts and wonders why they're all tail wringers. Don't pull a green colt's tail. He won't catch it on anything in the corral. When he's going well, pull it a little but don't pull it to the ridiculous point. Let him keep some of his natural fly-fighting ability.

There are a few points left for this chapter. One point concerns the stop and will be gone into more thoroughly in the next chapter.

The wild sliding stop that starts with a wide-open run and ends with flying dirt is better left to a horse further along in his training. A sliding stop can be made if speed is limited to a slow canter. Use all the same aids (rein, body, legs, voice) that you'd use for a set-and-turn but don't turn the colt. Hold him a second after the stop and then back him for a few steps.

Backing was something the colt learned when he was driven. He should be backed a few steps every ride. Keep your hands low. Use one rein at a time, never both. Get your weight off the seat of the saddle and squeeze with the legs at his every step. Reward him when he works correctly. Don't lose your temper; you can take the back-up off a colt very quickly. Hold him straight with your legs. Remember: he can't back straight if you sit in the saddle. You must get your weight off the saddle seat or he'll back like a snake.

Anything you do on horseback that requires the horse to get his hind legs up under him should be asked for with the rider's weight up off the seat and on the stirrups. His back must curve upward to have ease getting his hind legs forward. Any weight on his back at such times makes work difficult. The rider should get his weight forward for the slide, roll-back, the back-up, and the flying change of leads.

I like to rope. My colts get used to the lariat in basic training. A good time for this is when new things are occurring daily. One more new thing won't upset any sensible colt much. I build a loop and ride around the arena with it.

Stopping the colt, I swing it easy a few times. Then, if all goes well, I reward the colt for his trust in me. Before long I can build a loop and swing it any time I care to. My next step is to rope a light log and drag it around. The rope will pat the colt on the rump once in awhile, so the rider must be prepared for a little jumping around until the colt is used to this. Getting a colt used to the rope is basic. Roping stock is advanced training to be covered later.

Now, about hackamores. First, a hackamore, to me, means a rawhide noseband, braided rawhide over a rawhide core. I don't use hackamores braided over cable since such hackamores can't be shaped. Good hackamores can be purchased from most West Coast saddle shops. Hamley's, in Pendleton, Oregon, have fine colt gear. Severe Brothers Saddlery, Pendleton, Oregon, has top rawhide work because Duff Severe is one of the top braiders in this country. Carroll Saddle Company, McNeal, Arizona, has a complete line of fine hackamores made to the specifications of Ed Connell, author of *Hackamore Reinsman*, a fine book by a top horseman.

I shape a new hackamore for months before using it. My method of so doing is illustrated in the pictures. Sometimes, to prevent peeling the jaw on a very light-skinned colt, I wrap the sides with soft Canton cloth which is available at English saddle shops such as Miller Harness Company, and Kauffman's in New York.

Tying the hackamore reins (*riendas falsas*, meaning "false reins," for they're not permanently attached, just tied, also called *mecate*, which means "reins" and "lead rope") is easy once you know how. There should never be more than one wrap in front of the reins. Practice tying the reins following my illustration.

I don't like to use a *fiador* ("throatlatch") on colts I'm training because I feel that it hinders the action of the hacka-

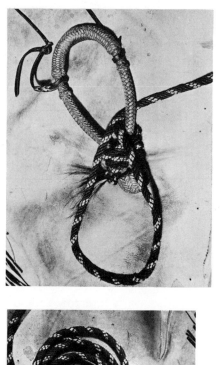
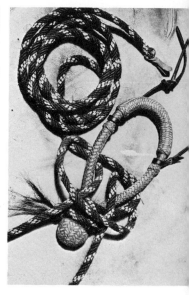

How to tie the reins on a hackamore.

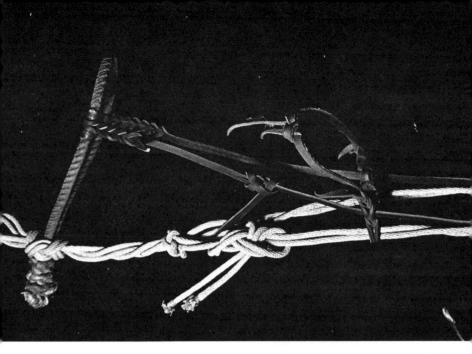

A rope hackamore with a *fiador* ("throatlatch").

more. The *fiador* is a good safety device to use when riding a snuffy colt out in the pasture. If he might spook and get away from you before the reins can be tied up, a *fiador* will save you a walk home and a loose horse. A good California mane-hair *fiador* is far better than the clothesline variety.

Hackamore training produces a colt ready to go straight up in the bridle. He has everything but collection—that is, he doesn't work the bridle yet. He knows how to work. After handling enough colts, the trainer has enough proficiency to accomplish his training tasks automatically and is ready to go on to produce top working colts. It's very difficult when you must stop and think about each individual action and wonder if you're doing things correctly. If your colt outworks other colts in your vicinity, you can't be doing too badly. Settle for *correct* slow work in the hackamore. Don't try to work yourself or your colt too fast.

89

X *Advanced Training: Bits and Reining*

If you've given your colt a good start, he won't be too tough to go on with. Many trainers can start a colt pretty well but have trouble keeping him going—that is, advancing him. A fine start can be made with the hackamore or snaffle bit, but things may fall apart when the colt goes into the finishing bit and he's neckreined.

The seasoned trainer has been meticulous in giving the colt a good start. We all know that this is extremely important. He's kept his hands low and has used the direct rein. He's pulled the colt into shape when he's fallen out of correct position. But when he's ready to finish the horse, the trainer may use a bit that has hardly advanced in design since the time of Alexander the Great. His hand position deteriorates from good to terrible. His fine working colt is soon a common sloppy horse working out of position, bouncing on stops, and traveling with a high head and a wild look in his eye. Ignorance and laziness have won again.

The main culprit is the neckrein. It's virtually impossible to keep a horse working properly when he's neckreined exclusively. The rein hand must be held either on the horse's withers in front of the fork of the saddle or above the horn. The former hand position allows almost no give-and-take with the horse's head, while the latter makes the rein hand way too high. Some trainers resort to tie-downs and running martingales. They are "gimmicking" their way around the problem. There is no way for a person using a curb bit and stock saddle to keep his horse in top form. The horse's work *must* deteriorate. A dressage horse will get better when being finished because the rider uses two hands on the reins and has no high fork and saddle horn to work around. This is straight talk—no beating around the bush. I also hasten to say that I'm speaking of reining horses, not self-workers such as cutting and roping horses.

There are a couple of ways to advance a colt in his training, and as a trainer I use both of these methods. First, I'm a trainer and want to train my horses to perfection. I scoff at no gear. I use a dressage saddle some of the time. On horses that don't have a good reining neck, this policy is excellent. It allows me to use very low hands.

Another training aid I use is a special bit, a California mouthpiece with provision for two reins. Since a horse should never be pulled with a curb bit, the extra rein allows me to pull a horse into position when he begins to work incorrectly. By keeping the horse working correctly, I keep him constantly improving.

The worst possible combination of gear you can put on a horse is a stock saddle with a seat sloping so excessively that it forces you back on the horse's kidneys—the weakest part of his back—and a grazing bit with split reins. I use saddles with level seats, stirrups hanging forward.

Many old-timers will scoff at the bit I use with two reins. "Can't ride with enough reins to handle a stage coach hitch," they say. Yet they will do a nice job on their colts with a *bosal* ("noseband"), a light *mecate*, and spade-bit reins. This combination is harder to hold and use than the Pelham bridle. I use the old California methods much of the time, as they do. Four reins are four reins, no matter whether they're mane hair or leather.

91

The methods are the same. When the Californian is teaching his colt to carry the spade, he uses a light *bosal* and small *mecate*. The colt carries a bit with no reins for a long time. Then reins are added, often tied on with light thread, and the colt is reined a little. He's five or six years old before he's straight up in the bridle and a well-trained horse.

These old-time trainers were and are wonderful. They knew what to do and took their time doing it. Most of their secrets were well kept, being handed down from father to son and friend to friend. The similarity between the training of Californian reinsman and the dressage trainer is striking. The end result is even more similar.

Arthur Konyot and I were good friends during the latter years of his life when he was riding for Arthur Godfrey. We played poker together a couple of times a week and were high on each other's abilities as poker players and horse trainers. I often worked horses at his arena (dressage riders say "school"), and he was amused with my training.

"Vot's dat you do der? A spin, you say? Ve call dot a pirouette. Votch dis!"—and he'd spin his dressage horse like a top.

"Dot's a rollback? I think it's a turn on de haunches"— and he'd execute a perfect rollback. I couldn't show him anything new except, maybe, roping a calf. Perhaps he liked me because he knew I thought so much of him both as a horseman and as a human.

I always admire a man who can do any skillful thing and is the best at it. Konyot was like that. He led an amazing life and was the best among perfectionists. He never bragged. He hardly ever talked about training horses, favoring poker as a topic of conversation.

His opinions were always of value to me, and I'd ask him about his ideas on how to correct a spoiled horse. I once had

The running martingale. This is a fine rig for bringing the horse's nose in. We also like using the regular rein in case the colt must be doubled.

a balker to train, and I asked him what he'd do. He watched the horse work, then said, "I tink I make him back oop until he vants to go ahead." I tried it, and it worked perfectly.

Watching Konyot work horses made me think more like he thought, and I started using many of his methods. My colts started working better right away. They got started California-style and then learned about pasture and trail riding. They learned about the rope and the cow. They learned to two-track (moving diagonally or sideways), run backwards, spin, roll back, and work in a fine, collected manner, which gave them a well-rounded education.

Lately I have read about West Coast horses having basic dressage training applied to them. I like this because there's no reason not to merge training methods and minds. We're all after a finely trained reining horse, and the best methods are needed.

Little has been said about the use of the snaffle bit during basic training. The reason for this is that I do very little basic snaffle-bit training, favoring the hackamore. I use the snaffle later on since the colt must eventually be bitted. Many top trainers start a colt in the snaffle bit. I don't get the results with it that I do with the hackamore. But not all colts work the hackamore, and these that don't should be trained in the snaffle. I've handled colts that could pull a freight train by their noses yet were fairly light in the snaffle.

There are various draw-rein affairs I sometimes use with the snaffle. The snaffle and running martingale make a good combination. I often use this rig with four reins, two of which fasten to the bit rings directly while the other two run through the rings of the running martingale. The martingale keeps the colt's head down.

If a colt gets "sticky"—that is, hard to turn or double— the draw rein is the answer. Long latigo reins are fastened to the cinch rings, run through the bit rings, then to the rider. This is a powerful rig that will unstick a spoiled colt and limber up a good one that's getting heavy in the hackamore.

Another form of draw rein fastens to the cinch between the colt's legs, then runs through the bit rings back to the rider. This rig is very good for colts that have a naturally bad head carriage, which is generally due to a conformation defect. The pull is down and in. Quite often nature's defect can be overcome with *much training*.

The regular draw rein. The rein is fastened to the cinch ring, runs through the colt's bit, and to the rider. The bit guard makes hurting the colt's mouth next to impossible.

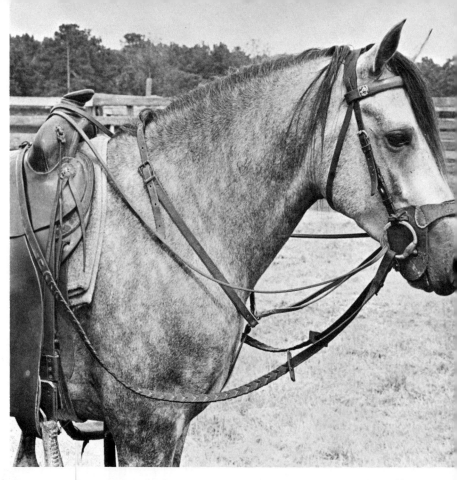

I call this the polo draw rein. The pull is down, bringing the colt's nose in. It's best used with a regular rein in case the colt must be doubled.

I make a special bit guard for the snaffle bit that makes the bit much easier on the colt. This guard buckles the mouth shut, while the bit can be raised toward the roof of the mouth, making it impossible for the colt to get his tongue over the bit. A buckle over the nose and a buckle under the chin provide the necessary adjustment.

When a colt gets his tongue over the bit, a lot of action soon follows. The colt will be walking along on a loose rein, head down and tongue playing with the bit. Suddenly he lunges straight up, perhaps falling over on his rider. The rider generally thinks that the colt is crazy, for he seemingly explodes with no reason. The reason is that he's worked his tongue over the bit and it's clanked down on the tender bars of his mouth. The rider compounds the mistake by hauling back on the reins, which increases the pain tremendously. So it stands to reason that the bit should be held up near the roof of the mouth. My bit guard does this. This special bit is available from Carroll Saddle Company.

Some people consider the spade bit a rough one, which it is if used by a person who doesn't understand its function. The high mouthpiece makes it virtually impossible for a horse to get his tongue over the bit. The roughest bit, in my estimation, is the broken snaffle with the extra long sidebars that is used on Tennessee Walking Horses. All that leverage makes it a jawbreaker—the small broken snaffle mouthpiece is jammed down on the bars with such force that the jaw can be easily broken.

We have almost no spade-bit tradition here in Florida, so we make no spade horses for resale. We do use a spade to mouth up colts. A wonderful head position is achieved in this manner.

There are expensive spade bits and cheap production-line spade bits. The cheap ones should be avoided like the plague.

A regular California spade bit is a work of art, made by master craftsmen who learned the trade in a father-to-son fashion. The bit must hang just right or it isn't comfortable to the horse. Cheap spade bits, ignorance, and bad reinsmanship have given the spade a reputation that it doesn't deserve.

The bit we use most of the time has the Salinas mouth. This is sort of a high curb, covered over with smooth copper, with a roller under the copper sheathing. The roller is made to produce a loud chirping noise and is called the cricket. A horse loves the taste of copper and enjoys making the cricket "chirp." It pacifies a colt.

Jack Carroll, of the Carroll Saddle Company, makes a bit for us with the Salinas mouth and a provision for the double reins. It is a great aid in getting colts started in the bridle and for correcting a bridle horse that goes out of position.

I think more importance is placed on the neckrein in North America than in any other part of the world. The perfect reining horse that can "turn on a dime" is something I've heard about all of my life, but I've seen none that I'd call perfect and mighty few that I'd call good. The California Reined Stock Horse and the trained dressage horse come closest to fitting the term perfection. The dressage horse works in fine fashion, but his maneuvers are slow. The stock horse works fast, but his mistakes happen in relation to his speed.

Almost all judges want to see speed in a reining horse. The run and the slide are generally executed at high speeds, forcing the horse to break his stop into a series of stops. He's trying to stop but is unable to because he'll dig in.

Monte Foreman does a fine job of explaining the stop, breaking it up into a series of three individual efforts from the wide-open run. He demonstrates that the horse must do this even when the rider is getting down fast, as is done dur-

Using a spade bit for a sliding stop. Dave Jones on Nan's Wimpy
Dude.

ing calf roping. His fine camera work demonstrates what actually happens at high speeds.

A horse can stop in one motion at high speeds but must do this on a prepared surface, such as tanbark over wet clay. I've stopped many a horse this way. The slide is a thrilling one to ride when the horse must ski thirty or more feet to stop.

The factors involved in stopping a horse are speed, the manner of ground, how the horse is trained, how he's ridden, and, of course, his natural ability.

Our ground is sandy here in Florida, and a horse jams into the ground very quickly. He must, as Foreman says, slide until he catches, go into the air, gather for another try, slide a bit, and go on eventually to end up in a slide. We don't practice this much, preferring never to run a horse wide-open unless he's working a cow or following a calf during roping practice. We do slide horses at slow speeds and slide them in one movement. The horse lopes, slides a few feet, and comes to a balanced stop.

This maneuver is easily executed on either a reining or a dressage horse. We are often able to train a colt to do this with no use of the reins whatsoever. First, I train the colt to stop from a walk. The colt is walked along a fence and is stopped. The cue is a tight quick squeeze with both legs. I rise in the saddle when I squeeze, and the colt soon learns to shoot both legs way up under himself. You can feel the back lower as the colt humps his back, allowing the legs to go up under. One rein is pulled and released at the same time leg pressure is applied. The colt is then either backed a few steps or turned into the fence to go back the way he came.

After some practice at this the colt will gather and get his legs up under himself at a slight squeeze of the rider's legs. The same aids are applied at a trot and, eventually, a canter. The colt will exhibit spectacular stops in one motion at a slow lope.

Many riders run the colt at a fence corner and stop him. He must stop or hit the fence. This does little to teach him to stop in other places and could make him dread the slide. A better practice is to lope in a large circle, gradually shortening until the circle is small. Finish it with a slow slide and a spin. The colt must be slightly collected in a tight circle; the collection aids the stop. Practice going both ways, but don't overwork.

Digressing for a moment, I gripe at excessive speed in reining classes. It seems that judges would much rather see speed than correct work. Speed is hard on a horse, and a lot of muscle is generally required to rein a horse at high speeds. The stops are bouncy, with the horse's head high and the mouth open. Horses are bent the wrong way in their circles, and most rollbacks are ridiculous. Of course, incorrect handling and training are a part of this, but speed is predominately at fault. I would far rather see better work than all that speed.

I'd also like to see a "free-style" reining in the manner of, say, Olympic figure skating. The horse would perform certain basic maneuvers but could stress what he's best at. This would be part regular reining, but a good showman who knows his horse could exhibit his skill to a high degree. Performing in time to music would make reining much more interesting to spectators.

A horse is out of position when he bounces to a stop with a high head. He's also out of position when his head is turned away from the direction in which he's going. He's not "following his head." His body is bent away from the direction he's going. He's not flexible. This condition is caused

101

mostly by complete use of the neckrein when no other aids are given. Generally the neckrein is used in a sloppy manner, hand held high, one rein tight, and the other loose—this actually forces the horse out of position.

Some horses naturally lope bent away from their lead— left lead, head to the right, body inclined to the right with the rump out, shoulders in. If you signal for a lead with legs on such a horse, the leg pressure will only serve to tighten the circle. Reverse leg pressure, and help from the reins is needed to straighten him out. This was previously discussed, but I must add that it's impossible to correct this horse with the indirect (neck) rein. He must be pulled with the direct rein.

People who own certain types of horses often ridicule others with different inclinations. Stock-saddle riders think an English rider is ridiculous. English riders are positive that users of stock saddles are crude, and they say so. Race-horse owners believe that other types of horses are next to worthless, speed being their only criterion.

I've been this way. Many years ago I considered an English saddle a toy, but today I frequently use my Passier dressage saddle to train the western horse. Why? I can maintain better hand position when I have no horn to contend with. Balance in a dressage saddle is good, though I'm not enough of a rider to breeze through a session on a bucking horse with one. I use both here—a well-trained horse is my goal.

Same thing with bits. I often use the double-rein bridle because a horse can be pulled on the top rein when he goes out of position. Jack Carroll and I designed a bit with provisions for the double rein. It has a Salinas mouth and a barrel cricket to pacify the horse. All we need to do if we want to look "western" is remove the top rein.

Production-line bits are now being made in this manner.

I don't see why they shouldn't work, though I personally prefer paying a little more for a handmade bit made by traditional bit makers. We have a little silver on our bits, which I personally like—on bits, yes, on saddles, no.

The English Weymouth bridle deserves some discussion. This rig consists of two bits, a snaffle, and a curb. Most horses work the English Weymouth better than they do an English Pelham. We use the Weymouth on all manner of horses well up in the bridle but never on a colt that needs a hard pull to the side, because the snaffle will be pulled into the colt's mouth if any force is used. Flexibility is excellent with the Weymouth because the individual bit may be used when needed. The horse can work the two bits in his mouth to create and keep a light mouth. This isn't true of the English Pelham.

Besides my Spanish Pelham, I use a soft rubber double-rein bit and the S-M Polo bit. The S-M Polo bit has a broad flat mouthpiece that never moves in the mouth, the curb action coming from the sidebars alone. These are both bits for horses with extrasensitive mouths; they are fine for this purpose.

And, of course, I use the spade bit. No finer bit is made for the *reinsman*. A horse will stay working better in the spade bit than in any other bit ever used as long as the rider knows his business. When circling, stopping, and spinning, the horse will work a little out of position, but his work is far superior to a horse being worked in other gear—*when being neckreined.*

The spade bit is good because it hangs well, better fills a horse's mouth (which is very large), has a good taste, and has a cricket for the horse's enjoyment. The horse works his tongue to chirp the cricket, makes mouth moisture, and stays much lighter than he would in the curb bit. Spanish reinsmen

103

feel that a horse must work his mouth on a bit to stay light. I agree.

A horse bitted with the common "grazer" doesn't work his tongue on the bit and makes no mouth moisture. Soon, just holding the stiff unyielding bit, his nose starts poking out. He throws his head up when stopped and travels in circles with his mouth pulled open and his head twisted away from his direction. He isn't following his head and is as inflexible as the bit he's carrying.

I rode such an animal for a friend. He'd purchased a nice Quarter Horse mare at a sale and wanted me to ride her for a month or so to see how she went. After I'd tried her, I was sure he'd gotten a real bargain.

This mare was highly trained in the hackamore. She did everything right. A slide was a sure thing every time I called for it. She'd spin until we were both dizzy, burying her pivot leg up to the fetlock in the sand. Broke to death!

What a difference there was when she worked in the bridle. She'd had a real top hand start her, but whoever put her in the bridle was as bad as her first trainer was good. She couldn't turn at all. When I asked her to circle at a lope she immediately came apart, her head bent abnormally away from her turn. She was dangerous; such a horse can easily fall.

When a horse is bent a little into his turn he "controls his ground." Circling correctly, the horse is handy, or "catty." When he is pulled out of position, the front legs can practically trip over a cigarette butt, and he can fall flat on the rider, always a dangerous happening. If the horse is circling to the left with his head pulled to the right and his whole body bent right, a slippery spot in the arena can cause a bad fall to the left.

So I told my friend about his mare and advised him not

104

to use her. She was a bit old to retrain economically. She was bred and raised a fine filly.

The horse correctly trained for the spade bit has years of hackamore training and is used double rein (*bosal* plus bit) when initially bitted. He's in the bridle and *bosal* (small noseband, small rope reins), and can be pulled when working out of position. He has years to learn good work. Combine a poor bit with a poor reinsman, give the animal no time to learn the work, and the result is always a fouled-up horse.

The handling horse, whether he is called a reined stock horse, a reining horse, or a dressage horse, is my idea of a finished product. Pleasure horses, trail horses, and roping and cutting horses receive specialized training which had fairly broad coverage in my earlier book, *Practical Western Training*. We'll rehash a little here.

Pleasure, trail, and cutting, as horse-show classes, seem to go through various phases. Something is popular for a while; then it's out.

Pleasure-horse classes used to feature an unnaturally slow lope on an excessively loose rein. Trainers would practice this slow lope until their horses were actually brainwashed. The horse would do a slow lope for hours. I guess that no bridle was needed because the rider never picked up a rein. A horse trained in this fashion was practically useless. When asked to do anything else, he'd pop his head up and refuse to rein—but judges would make such a horse a class winner. The situation had to change, and it did.

First, the judges called for a rein pulled up enough so that the rider had some measure of control. Then, wonder of wonders, the lope was sometimes called for. If the horse couldn't be controlled after loping around the ring a few times, he was out. Pleasure classes are now so big and tough that a horse must have some ability and training to win. When fifty horses are in a class, a missed lead will often put the horse out of the ribbons.

Horses we train for pleasure are trained the same as we train a reining horse, only we don't carry advanced training as far. A horse with too much cue in him will be a little high for a pleasure class. Leads are worked on quite a bit, and we want a nice, comfortable, relaxed stop. A slow walk-around pivot on the hind legs is a must and not hard to get with most horses. We want a supple horse but also a relaxed one. A horse is loped quite a ways when we do lope, perhaps half a mile at a time, but this is done on the trails in the woods rather than in a ring. This doesn't brainwash a horse.

Many people might think us funny, but we actually train trail horses on our trails. We have water-filled ditches to cross, gullies to ride through, logs to jump, and wild creatures that spook horses, such as quail, deer, and turkey. A really specialized trail horse must learn to pack deer, bear, and so on, but this is hardly ever done in day-to-day training. Sometimes a trail horse (the show variety) is asked to walk over a cowhide or bearskin. He can be trained for this by making him stand on a similar object when eating. I feel that this method has the tendency to brainwash a horse. When we approach a rattlesnake or water moccasin, I'd just as soon my horse wouldn't walk all over it, so I don't favor brainwashing. Not being too smart and alert, I like my horse to take care of me back on the trail.

XI *Advanced Training: Roping*

A roping horse is definitely a specialist. He needs very good basic training to the point where a rider can put him where he wants him when he wants him there. He must be a sensible horse, for the roper's box can be a dangerous place on a screwball. It's easy enough for a smart horse to get tangled in a rope. Give me plenty of common sense in my rope horse.

As I said earlier, I like to rope, so I swing a rope and catch old rubber buckets and light logs right from the start. The colt should learn that the rope won't hurt him and not to fear it. The rope should be played with all through basic training, though I don't favor catching stock until the colt is well trained.

It's a good plan to get the young colt used to the roper's box if you have time for such extra work. I like to take a rubber feed tub to the box and feed the colt there. During his long training period he should be tied in the box for a rest. If it seems like another stall to him, he'll never dread it as much as a colt would without this training.

A rope horse must rate (track) cattle well, so his first association with stock should be to rate them. No rope is used for this. The colt is loped up in back of a slow calf and held there. A large safe lot is better for this than the arena is because calves shouldn't be run out of the box for some time. It's good, however, if you can ride the colt by the box and pens to help another roper load calves for roping.

Ken Serco on Ginger, introducing her to the feeling of weight on the rope by pulling a light log.

The prospective roping horse should have regular pasture and trail riding to make a horse of him—a sensible useful horse. Cow work is a help. Some rating of calves every few days is enough. He should hold his place, not run up on the calves. Ten to twelve feet back of a calf is where I like to rope, so I hold the colt there. Three calves a day are plenty. When a calf starts to get hot, stop the colt and pick another calf. Moving cattle from pasture to pasture is good work, as is checking pastures. The rope horse is sort of a cow horse, so all the bovine association he can get is good for him.

When the colt can rate a calf pretty well in the lot, work can be moved to the arena. I think breakaway roping is good for the colt at this stage because he knows the lariat won't hurt him and he knows a bit about rating cattle.

Lope up behind a slow calf and follow it until it slows down and the colt is rating just right. You're carrying your rope ready. If all goes O.K., swing your rope easy and, if things continue to go O.K., rope the calf, follow it at the same rating position, and pull the rope off (break it away). Don't stop the colt. He should continue to follow until he's slowed down by the rider. You don't want him setting up every time you rope a calf, for this is all ahead of him. Now, if he spooks at the rope when you rate the calf, don't rope yet. Follow a couple more calves with your loop slowly swinging until he settles down.

I'd break away for a month or so if he does all right at it. My next step is to dally-rope the calf. This means that I'll rope a calf, dally my lariat around the saddle horn, and gradually slow the calf down. I stay on the colt and have someone turn the calf loose for me. I'll dally-rope as many calves as I would catch with my breakaway loop.

I can soon rope a calf, dally up short, get off with the end of my rope, and turn the calf loose myself. If anything goes

109

Paco gives Dave Jones a hand in legging down a calf.

wrong, I can turn the dallies loose and stay out of a storm.

If the horse is to be a ranch horse, his training is about finished when he becomes a dally horse. Practice makes perfect, and soon the colt will rate, let you rope, run up for you to dally short, and stand while you doctor the calf or whatever you want to do. If he handles well, there will be little trouble roping heels. In fact, if you have to rope heavy stock, you should heel from the colt rather than head. By heeling rather than heading, you don't have to run the colt so fast or handle as much weight.

The heel loop is a trap loop. The header makes his catch, dallies up short, stops, and comes back, dragging the steer. You ride your heeling horse to the left of the steer, a few feet behind it. The loop is thrown so that the back half of the loop slaps the steer over the hocks while the front half flips around in front of the hind legs to form a trap. The steer

110

is dragged into the trap, slack is jerked, dallies taken, and the steer is laid down and stretched out. Heeling is fairly easy if the header is good.

Dally roping (*dar la vuelta*) is becoming increasingly popular in such states as Colorado, New Mexico, and Arizona. I still have people tell me that they'd rather risk their necks than their hands. The art isn't that difficult. After roping the stock and jerking up your slack, the first and most important thing to do is to turn your hand over on the rope, bring the rope to your horn, and dally with the heel of your hand down, thumb up. Then slip your hand down the rope until the hand is back near your hip. Practice on something like a rubber bucket or an old milk can. Such an object is light enough that you can't get a finger cut off in the rope from lack of experience. I like to lope by a milk can, rope it, jerk slack, and dally as I go by. This is good practice, because you have to be fast and accurate to dally on anything not moving while you lope by. This is also a very good way to get a colt used to the rope and the act of dallying.

It's a waste of time to write about hard-and-fast single-steer roping. This is something best learned from a top hand. Oklahoma is the home base for steer ropers, because, I've heard, it's tall-grass country. It's almost impossible to heel a steer in tall grass. I've roped and busted steers by myself but am not high on it. It's hard on horses, stock, and cowboys. When a rank steer gets up on the fight, the cowboy's in trouble. At the least it's a foot race.

Team tying is also a little rough. I hate to see a steer almost jerked apart, as often happens. I love dally roping, but I just tie my rope for calves.

Good ol' calf roping. I've roped a jillion of them and enjoyed my last calf as much as I did my first. I started in a funny way. I'd never been interested in calf roping. It wasn't my cup of tea. I was a colt breaker and horse trainer. True, I was a pretty fair roper and could catch a calf, but that was the extent of it. I'd dally-roped a lot of steers but had never specialized at calf roping.

Back in 1954, I was living and training in the Northeast. Visiting a buddy nearby, I found he'd gone to a four-go-round rodeo. I went over to find out how he was doing. Finding him back of the chutes, I inquired, as a topic of conversation, how the calf roping was going. "Mighty poor," was his reply. "Nobody's tied one down yet."

It took a few minutes for this to sink into my hard head. When I found out that he actually meant that no one had made any time at all, I said, "Ol' buddy, as of this minute, right now, I have just become a calf roper. How 'bout the loan of your horse?"

There were two events for ropers, calf roping and ribbon roping. The ribbon roping as practiced there was a two-man event. The roper caught the steer, and a mugger grabbed it. The roper then dismounted and tied a ribbon to the steer's tail.

I entered both events for the remaining three go-rounds and won the ribbon-roping each time. I had a first, a second, and a no-time with the calf roping, and there I was, a top roper, on a borrowed horse. I paid my buddy one-fourth the winnings and then and there thought a lot more about roping.

Roping was just starting in the region, and no one knew much about it. I was as unpolished as anyone could be, but I had a better start than most because I could catch a calf. With dollar signs in both eyes, this dally roper tied on hard and fast.

A fellow owed me a big board bill for an old Quarter mare so I dunned him for the money. He said he'd rather let me have the horse than pay the bill. I agreed, and I was lucky, for she was an old Hancock mare, a bloodline hard to beat for roping. The ol' gal had no handle to speak of, but I had all of a cold, snowy winter to work her.

A good arena was a must. I wanted a big one, because I knew I needed to practice on turning, twisting calves. I settled for one 150 by 300 feet. I built the chutes so that I could turn out my own calves.

I found some nice, light Angus calves. I wanted the black calves, because they hold their heads much lower than the common Brahma and are much harder to rope. Their short, muscular legs make for a difficult tie, but they're fine for practice.

The mare liked the work and made a good rope horse for that country. Her stop was too soft for a top rope horse, but she was perfect as a practice horse.

I went through several phases before settling on a certain style. It seemed easier to rope around the horse's neck, rating slightly to the right of the calf. The drawback to this method soon became obvious. First, it's unnatural for a horse to rate cattle either to the right or to the left. A bad result is that the horse must take a severe pull from his neck rope if he is not directly behind the calf. This teaches the horse to swing off (duck off) when the roper dismounts, an inconvenient and often dangerous occurrence.

Many rope horses duck off. This bad habit could stand some discussion. The slap of the taut rope is generally the cause. A right-handed roper's horse will get slapped on the right side of the neck, causing a bad duck-off to the left. The dismounting roper will get off into his horse's front legs, or, get hit, head to head. A great many ropers have been injured in this fashion.

The practice of using a chain instead of a neck rope contributes to the problem. A neck rope set high up near the throatlatch will force the rope to punish the horse. A loose neck rope will help. Roping straight behind the calf will help. Dally roping, for a while, will help, for the roper stays on the horse and can hold him straight. Roping light calves will help. Getting off slow and late and holding the horse straight will perhaps cure the habit.

If the habit is truly confirmed, try some big calves and pitch the slack in the rope over the horse's head so that the rope will slap tight on the near side. Stop the practice and rope some light calves with a loose neck rope when results are achieved.

I gradually learned to catch my calf from a position right behind him. Immediately my mare started jerking calves better. My dismount was bad because I hurried too much. I finally learned to stay in my stirrup until the calf was jerked. My weight in the stirrup helped my mare handle the calf. Leaving to shape up a calf took a lot of practice—you don't run down there just any old way.

To leg down or flank? That is the question. Since the calves we roped there were generally pretty big, I legged down most of them.

After dismounting, the roper gets his right arm over the rope on the way to the calf. If the calf is up and moving, it must be blocked. If the roper gets behind in his leverage while shaping the calf up, the little critter will pull him all over the arena. So the roper should stay in very close to his rope and get there fast, but in a controlled manner. It is no use going so fast that you fall all over the calf. Approaching the calf, the roper should hold his arm out and down so that his arm will contact the calf's right foreleg. He then grabs the foreleg above the dewclaw and reaches for the flank skin with his left hand. The straighter he holds the calf's leg the more leverage the roper has. The calf is lifted up and against the taut rope, which furnishes the leverage for the throw. A yearling—even a light steer, can be thrown in this manner.

As the calf is thrown, the roper should pop the piggin' string on the foreleg, cross the calf, and force the hind legs up and over the foreleg with his right leg. The foreleg is pulled back with the tie rope, while the hind legs are forced forward by the roper's leg. If the calf is big, the tie may need to be "sneaked" on. This means that the roper must get one wrap as easily, quietly, and quickly as possible. Then another wrap is taken—"two wraps and a hooey." The hooey is a half hitch. After two wraps are taken, the roper lays his hand, palm up, over the wraps. The third wrap is taken over the hand, and the end is picked up with the ends of the fingers and pulled under the third wrap. This makes a half hitch. There's no other way to tie a fast half hitch.

Kids (and their elders) can go to roping schools nowadays and learn all this. I had to learn it by roping many calves. My ground work was my biggest headache. I could do things on a horse, but getting over my awkwardness on the ground took some doing.

I learned a lot at the shows. Roping at home was easy because I knew my calves. This calf runs to the fence. That calf digs in and sprints to the catch pen. But at the shows the calves were strangers.

At one roping club there was a Brangus heifer that had never been tied. I really dreaded her, but I knew I had to get her someday. I figured out my strategy. I'd rope her, ride up close, stop hard, get down, and get to her as fast as possible.

One day I drew her, and everything went wrong. She didn't run. She loped and looked back at me. When I caught her, she got no jerk at all because I was dumb enough to get off on my reins and because the mare propped instead of setting down.

115

That heifer did everything to me but kill me. First she ran past me wide open, and the rope flattened me. Next time I jumped over it, but I couldn't touch her. Finally she tangled me up so badly she dragged me twenty feet by my leg. Then the ol' mare gave up, and calf and horse loped off, leaving me a flattened, wrecked mess.

Some fellow (I'll be forever thankful to him) yelled, "Whoa!" from the grandstand, and the mare slammed up, giving the heifer her first good jerk. I managed to get there, grab a leg, flop her, and make the tie.

As horse and I sheepishly left the arena amid the din of a thousand horse laughs, I heard my buddy say, "Gosh, I shoulda loaned you my horse. You'da had it easy." I wanted to club him but didn't have the energy. Next week he drew the same heifer and left the arena, vomiting, on his hands and knees, horse down, wrapped in the lariat, with cowboys trying to cut the horse loose.

I made a few bucks at every little show I went to and improved with practice and experience. What really helped my roping was a cow outfit in Virginia. Those guys loved rope horses, and I roped all day every day. I don't think I was really a calf roper before working for this outfit. I got so I could catch any calf I could reach with my rope.

Nowadays I rope in spurts. Sometimes I have a few rope horses to train and get good at it. But they always seem to arrive during the heat of the summer here in Florida. This is tough, where summers are so hot and humid. I'll be out of shape, smoking too much, and carrying too much weight for a lot of calf roping. One calf isn't bad, but roping and tying down calves hour by hour is exhausting work even for the most fit. You need to be in perfect physical condition to rope a lot of calves.

Anyone learning to rope shouldn't attempt to train rope

horses, because the trainer must be able to catch calves any-time he throws his loop. The fledgling roper should practice on foot, roping the far end of a bale of hay until he can catch the bale every time. Stand a bale of hay on edge and get twelve feet directly behind it. Throw hard every time. I find *I'm* best when I use very little wrist motion. The loop goes farther, straighter, and flatter. If you can throw hard, jerk slack properly, and catch the far end of that hay bale every time, you are ready to start roping from a horse.

A good, reliable practice horse is a must to learn on. There are many such horses around. Spread the word that you want one, and you'll hear from folks. If you're not in roping coun-try, put a "horse wanted" ad in a horse magazine, such as *Western Horseman* or *Quarter Horse Journal.*

A practice horse must be reliable and gentle. No one can learn to rope off a colt or a screwball. Many fine rope horses can be found that just aren't fast enough or that stop too soft for a contest horse. Don't worry about age if the horse is sound. Forget speed. You want a horse that will rate well, stand quietly in the box, and work a rope. Look for a better horse only after you're completely consistent on your original practice horse. If roping is just a hobby you practice with your buddies, this may be all the horse you need.

Perhaps, roping with friends, you find that you're the slow man. Some of your buddies may rope in seventeen seconds while you're roping in twenty-five seconds. Your first thought might be that you need a better horse. This is probably wrong. You need to improve your technique. Of course, if you're earnest, your friends may give you some tips. A very good way to find your faults is to have someone take movies of you in action. View these movies at normal speed, then in slow motion. You'll generally find your mistakes to be your method of approaching, throwing, and tying the calf.

117

Do you flank? If so, your method of getting under the rope is important. You need to go under the rope immediately after stepping off because the rope is higher off the ground close to the horse. Perhaps you're running too fast and can't control your actions when you get to the calf. Smoothness is essential. You should hold the rope with your left hand, reach over and grab flank with your right, lever the calf up, and drop him smoothly against the rope, using your rope for leverage to aid the throw. String the foreleg, push up the hind legs, and make a smooth, quick tie. Being smooth is more important than being rapid. Try watching yourself on film in slow motion. This is an easy way to spot rough, uneven movements.

So eventually you improve and are capable of tying fast calves. You decide to train your own rope horse. The steps I've previously outlined will hold true if you remember a few points:

1. Don't rush your colt. He won't be a top rope horse until he's six or seven years old. If you're patient, he could stay good until he's twenty-five.

2. Don't always rope off of your contest horse. When he's at his best, leave him alone. Use your practice horse for practice.

3. Box work can make or break you. When training your colt, make him like the box. Control him in the box. Let some calves out, but don't chase them. Teach him to score when *you* want him to. Let six calves out and rope one contest-style. Let three come out, and hold the colt in the box. He'll want to come out when the chute gate bangs open. Just don't chase every calf you let out.

4. Breakaway roping is good. You don't want your horse setting up every time you rope. He should wait until you get

down. Breakaway roping will keep him from "scotching" (laying back, or stopping too soon). Dally roping is also very good.

5. You can rope without using the box. Just ride out with the calves and chase and rope one. Teach your horse to short-cut to a calf, then to rate it consistently.

6. The calf horse does most of the work by himself. You can rope off of a good horse without a bridle. So don't rein him all the time and don't get off on your reins (jerk the reins as you step off). Teach him to set up when you shift your weight and put your left hand on his neck.

7. Learn to jerk slack and throw it away correctly. I throw my slack straight up. Throw it some place so the colt will never step in it. Always carry a *sharp* pocketknife. If you miss your slack, your colt may step over the rope and get wound up. It's better to get him loose fast than to cripple him. *Never tie a rope on your horn unless you have a sharp knife in your pocket.* It's a common joke around here that I always carry a big, sharp pocketknife. It wears my Levi's out before their time, and the boys have various ideas why I keep that big knife razor sharp. We know, don't we?

8. Your rope horse must be shod. The kind of shoes he wears should be determined by his natural stop and the ground he'll be used on. If he slides too far to jerk a calf, he should wear calks on his shoes. If he sticks his legs in the ground, plates are the answer. He should always be equipped with skid boots because the wear and tear on a horse's back fetlocks is terrific. When you use skid boots and see how they get torn up, you'll always use them if you care about your horse.

9. Tie-downs are in general use on roping horses, and, in time, you'll probably have to use one. It should be fitted as loosely as possible because a horse can't run as well in a tie-

down as he can with a free head. It's almost impossible to handle the reins perfectly when roping calves, so don't be surprised if the horse's head starts up. You can help him by using an easy bit and not getting down on your reins. A running martingale is fine to help keep his head down, but it's just one more thing to get the rope fouled in. When using a tie-down on a rope horse, use a gentle one that he can lean into.

10. Many beginning ropers use their regular saddles and are skimpy with blankets. This is a mistake. A rope horse needs a lot of protection on his back. The shock of a lot of calf roping will make him sore. The back cinch should be snug but can be adjusted. If he's working too much rope (backing up too much and choking the calf), loosen the back cinch. The saddle will tip up, pinch his withers, and he'll hold. If he needs to work more rope, tighten the back cinch. I use two doubled Navaho blankets and a pad when roping, and my saddle is broad enough to accommodate all of this.

11. I use a back-up line on my rope-horse prospect to teach him to work a rope. *I don't hit him in the face with my slack*! When starting a colt working the rope, I attach a clothesline rope to the light *bosal* under the bridle, run it to a little pulley on the fork of my saddle, and carry the rest. The rope is as long as the lariat, so I have plenty of control out to the end of the rope. When the colt is working the rope a little, I shorten the clothesline rope to about ten feet and pull him back a few steps as I start to the calf. I don't want him to work too much. If he keeps backing up when I want to tie the calf, he'll choke it, and the kicking calf is hard to tie.

Remember the mistakes ropers make so that you won't make them:

1. Don't rope calves all the time on a finished horse.
2. Don't chase every calf out of the box.
3. Don't hit your horse with the rope.
4. Don't forget to carry a sharp knife.
5. Don't rope without skid boots.
6. Don't get off on the reins unless absolutely necessary.
7. Don't lend your horse to everyone who asks.
8. Don't forget that breakaway and dally roping help.
9. Don't make your horse hate the box.
10. Don't rush your horse in his training.

XII *Advanced Training: Cutting*

Everyone seems to like a good cutting horse. Cutting was a novelty twenty years ago and is now a tremendously popular sport. Cutting-horse competition is competition at its finest and can be enjoyed by children, teenagers, and business-men, as well as by professional horsemen. There are enough classes for everyone.

Californians used to call a cutting horse a "trick horse made in Texas." Some notable California pioneers, such as Dan Dodge and Bill Elliot, were soon contesting and doing well. Finally, cutting has made great progress in the domain of the California Reined Stock Horse.

The cutting horse is quite an animal. A top one is spectacular at his work. I don't know how anyone can watch such a horse and not admire him. Even die-hard exponents of English riding gather in the stands to watch cutting.

There are two ways to train a cutting horse. One way is to take a natural prospect and teach him to enjoy his work. The other method is to make him dread not working. I think that more horses are trained by the latter method than by the former. Truthfully, both methods intermingle a little.

A cow horse, after all, is a horse with a horse's inclinations to be lazy. The most willing prospect will goof off and require punishment to get him straightened out. A horse will slow down on set-and-turns, getting behind his cattle. He must be spurred fairly hard to keep him alert and heading cattle.

122

Starting a filly cutting cattle indoors.

Spurring a cutting horse isn't generally the same easy "extension of the leg aid" one would give a reining horse. But a firm hit with a blunt spur isn't the same as tearing the shoulders up, a method many trainers employ to teach horses to duck and dodge with a cow.

Most horse owners object to having a wide-eyed quivering hulk of horseflesh turned back to them as a finished horse. Many horses dread the cow, while others fear not working the cow because they know they'll be hurt if they don't work.

Cruel methods are often used in cutting-horse training, and gimmicks are sometimes used right up to show time. A trainer will enter the arena with a chain behind the horse's ears, tying his head down until it's time for him to cut. The trainer will run the horse, setting him up a few times to let him know the chain's there. He will then remember to keep his head down when working.

123

Cap Bar works hard to keep a heifer from the herd. Dave Jones up.

And such a trainer may spur, one side and then the other, to get the horse jumping back and forth before showing in the hope that he'll continue to jump back and forth in front of the cow. This mechanical "jumping jack" will often duck and dodge when the cow is standing still.

The National Cutting Horse Association has made it plain that such actions are not condoned. True, a rider can't use gimmicks or spur excessively in the show ring, but many trainers seem to disregard the audience. People see cruelty, and cruelty to cutting horses has done a lot to hurt the sport. More people now say: "Don't train at the shows. Train your horse at home." My personal feeling is that cruelty isn't needed in cutting-horse training. I don't feel that occasionally hitting a horse in the shoulder with a dull spur is cruelty. A horse will dope off, bounce a couple of times before turn-

124

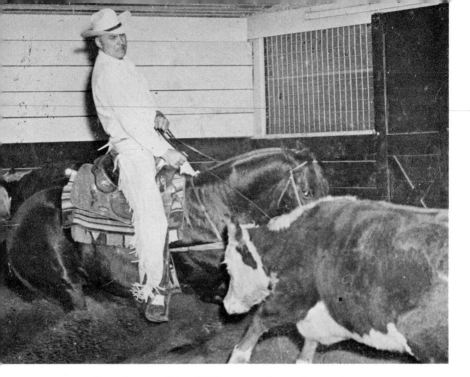

Dave Jones and Steel Helmet practice cutting cattle.

ing, and will lose a cow. Hitting him *lightly* on the shoulder after his front feet hit the ground isn't cruel, but tearing him up with sharp spurs *is* cruel.

The cow horse must head his cattle or they'll run on forever without turning. Spurring back of the cinch will make him run a bit faster to head the cow. This isn't cruel.

The cow horse can be made dull by overwork. A novice cutting horseman will almost always overwork his horse. It's fun for him, so he cuts cow after cow in practice. The horse gets tired, falls behind his cow, and gets the spirit spurred out of him for being tired. Three cows are enough for a trained horse. If the horse is too fresh, he should be ridden down a bit, and just plain riding will suffice. He shouldn't be worked down on cattle.

This makes training difficult. The colt needs work on a

125

specific problem but gets worn down before he can get much correction. I've never used a mechanical calf, but I believe that such a device would be excellent for quick work on specific problems.

General riding and ranch work are excellent to keep a cow horse well trained. Moving cows from pasture to pasture, roping cattle for doctoring, and checking pastures are all fine in that they furnish variety and tend to keep the colt interested. Riding through a bunch of cows and cutting one out to check her is topnotch work for a colt.

Training the cutting horse is thoroughly discussed in *Practical Western Training,* so there's little use going into general aspects of training. Some special problems I've come up with when training cow horses should be discussed here: (1) charging, (2) heading a cow on the fence, (3) falling back too much (guarding the herd), (4) laneing cattle, and (5) keeping the training you have (not letting the horse go downhill).

Most colts will charge until they've learned to stay back to keep their leverage. Some trained horses charge just because they feel good. Steel Helmet, pictured in *Practical Western Training*, needs a lot of stiff trail riding before he settles down to cow work. His silliness needs to be worked out before he's a cow horse. King of Clubs, another horse mentioned in that book, needs very little work and will sour on steady cutting. So, it seems, one needs to know the horse.

To keep a charging colt back, the rider must handle him by pulling him, as easily as possible, to the correct position. Letting the colt run up on cattle teaches him nothing. He'll soon understand the leverage he gains by staying back. When he controls a cow easily by leverage, it'll dawn on him that getting too close means a lot of hard work.

Many trainers intentionally allow a colt to get too close,

losing the cow. They then ride hard to get around it before it reaches the herd. They think that this will teach the colt to stay back and watch. This works on some colts but makes race horses out of others. I think it's the long way around a problem.

When forcing the colt to the desired position, steady reining isn't desirable. The trainer must use leg aids and a pull and release on the reins, because the cutting horse shouldn't be taught to rely on his rider. An easy hackamore is best. Padding the bit with rubber is another good choice. If the colt's head goes way up when he's reined, some form of tiedown should be used, but it must be discarded as soon as the colt learns how to work.

Sour cattle will teach a colt to charge. Ideal conditions aren't always with us. Some cattle sour quickly. It might go like this. The trainer has fifteen cows that gentle quickly. Some do and some don't. He knows better than to use these cattle, because a horse must be right on top of them to work. But a colt's owner pays a visit and wants to see his colt work. The trainer hates to say no and hates to admit his cattle are not good. So he brings the herd in, saddles the colt, warms him up, and rides in to cut. The colt must get on top of the cows to move them at all. He shows nothing. The owner is disappointed, and the trainer knows that he's made a bad mistake.

This is the difficult thing about cutting-horse training. You need gentle cattle to start a colt on and ranker cattle after he knows how to work. The colt knows that he's in the arena to work and will go up so close to work a played-out cow that he'll remember the experience and want to work up close. Running cattle are just about as bad. If a cow runs wide open from arena fence to arena fence, the colt must run wide open to head her. This cow is just as sour as a "dead-head"

127

because she's next to impossible to turn and will wear out a colt in a few minutes.

Inside arenas spoil cattle. When they see no daylight, they seem to give up. One winter in Colorado we gentled 150 head of cattle to the point of no work at all.

There's no real solution. Some suggestions are: don't overwork your cattle; don't furnish your cattle for "cutting bees"; learn enough about cattle to know when you're about to sour a cow; have enough cattle so that a group can be rested; change cattle often; buy a ranker type such as the Brahma; and use calves for roping and cutting. The last suggestion works pretty well if you have one rope horse and one cutting horse, both trained, that need very little work. You can use one set of calves all season.

Sixty calves should last a trainer a long time. There is a heavy initial investment, but, if they are bought right and sold right, little or no money should be lost. Such a number of calves allows frequent rest periods, so they will last longer. Of course, a trainer with a large number of horses to work may need a much larger herd to work from. A mechanical calf would save cattle and contribute greatly to cutting-horse training.

The horse will probably be a little weak when picking a cow off the fence. The horse should be head-to-head for a safe block. He must run parallel with the cow if she's moving with any speed. He can't block well when parallel because the sour cow will go under the horse's neck, especially at the fence. The cow horse should run parallel until he gets a bit ahead of the cow, though the horse's head should angle in toward the cow. When he gains his advantage, he must block ahead of her to turn her. When she turns, the maneuver must be performed from the other direction. The colt is then boxing in his own cow as he'd do on the range. This is hard work on a fast cow that's hard to turn. The cutter should get rid of a bad-running cow as soon as possible when showing because he gains nothing from working such an animal. Owning such cattle will do nothing but turn your cutting prospects into race horses.

The colt stays slightly ahead of a good cow, blocking her every turn. If she blocks easily, she'll duck and dodge. Such play earns a high score; a charging, rank, hard-to-hold cow will test a horse and is generally very good for high scoring. An otherwise good horse is often afraid of the fence. Some trainer, at some time, has forced him into it, and he's afraid to work too tight and will lose a rank cow by being out of position, letting her get by under his neck. An old horse that's afraid of the fence is almost impossible to reschool.

Teaching a colt or reschooling a horse to block on the fence requires supplying the horse and having some good cattle and/or a mechanical calf. Easy cattle that will turn from a horse will give him confidence. Being able to work the horse over to the fence and hold him there with hand and leg aids will show him where to be.

The horse must run with the cow, but, upon approaching the fence, he must move his rear over until he's parallel with the fence, facing the cow. Many horses will do this but will jump away from the fence, allowing the cow to go on through the hole he's vacated. After the horse becomes responsive to leg aids, he'll get over and hold his position if the cow isn't moving too fast, isn't too rank, and turns away from him rather than trying to force through. So, you see, you need good cattle to teach a colt or reschool a sour horse.

If you use a turnback man, he should know how to fade back and not press a cow so hard that she'll bull right through. Yell at your turnback if he's coming on too strong (at home, I mean).

129

Again, the mechanical calf should be a big help because it can be made to move as slow as is desired, and the maneuver can be repeated time after time, slowly, to teach the colt to block on the fence.

Most good colts learn what leverage can do to ease their work and will fall back too much. They'll move back so much that they get right in the herd. You can't really show a colt when he's in this stage of learning. He's "guarding the herd."

In general, I think it's a big mistake to spur a colt to move him up. He'll usually just fall back more and stick in the herd. The dogger's bat is a better answer; a few whacks over the rump will generally move him up. Pet the colt when he responds and moves up to where you want him.

A fast-running cow is prone to "laneing" (running the lane between the cutter and the turnback man). This type of cow will teach a colt to run alongside, never heading, for it's terrifically hard work to head, head again and again when working a fast-running, hard-to-head cow. Getting the colt over the habit requires cattle that are slower and turn better. Later, when you get a fast cow, head her a couple times and get off her. The colt needs to know how to set up such a cow but will certainly sour if used on such an animal too much.

A colt will often learn to use the fence to make his blocks for him. He knows the cow must turn, so he lays back, waiting for her to reach the fence. Since the fence creates a problem, the solution for the rider is to get the horse away from the fence. This means pasture or large arena cutting. In the pasture the colt soon learns that he had better set up the cow or he'll be chasing her all over the landscape. With all this room to work he learns to shape up a cow much better than he would in an arena. Care must be taken not to spoil a colt with overwork in the pasture, for a rider can get carried away.

130

It's better to make a couple of blocks and quit than to tire the colt to the point of exhaustion.

If no pasture is available, working sideways in a large arena will often help. If your arena is one hundred by three hundred feet, use the three-hundred-foot part as the side, rather than the length.

It's often the case that the colt will show great promise, only to slide downhill rather than make the good finished cow horse that he should. This is almost always the fault of the rider, for we all like to cut cattle and tend to do too much of it. A finished horse doesn't need to cut cattle every day. Once in a while is enough. You can take almost any horse that has gone downhill, rest him for a few months, and go into the arena and cut in fine fashion for a couple of minutes. This horse wants to cut cattle but thinks that he'll get tired if he's kept at it. Show him some consideration and he'll come back. Rest him, work him lightly, and he'll cut cattle. Overwork him, and he's through. Ride him on the trails and in the pasture for exercise but don't overexercise him on cattle.

It takes a mighty will power to keep from overworking a horse. A lady I knew liked to haul her horse and cut in strange arenas. She always paid her way, insisting on paying a little money for "cow feed." She would haul her horse forty miles, saddle up, warm up the horse, and cut for only two to three minutes. Her horse stayed working. She had the guts to know when to stop.

Horses like to cut cattle as well as people do. Tire out a man or a horse, and both sour. A fresh horse used occasionally will enjoy cutting cattle and will stay good until he's retired.

If you like cutting horses you'll certainly want to belong to the National Cutting Horse Association. It doesn't cost too much to belong. Twenty-five dollars will get you in, and fifteen dollars a year will keep you in. You'll get a booklet with rules to abide by and information about how to put on a show. You'll receive *Cutting Hoss Chatter* monthly, which gives show dates and show results and keeps you informed about who's doing what. Staying a member in good standing means not cheating, not fighting or creating an uproar at shows, and behaving yourself in a normal manner. Be a good horseman and a good sport.

There are a lot of trials and tribulations while making a colt into a cutting horse. It's expensive, because keeping cattle is expensive. Keeping good, fresh cattle costs money, and it's about the only way to come out on top. If you like cutting enough, the joys of owning a top horse and winning with him will make up for the expense and work. Hope you have the next world's champion.

XIII *Ground Handling*

A friend of mine recently said, "I've read just about every training book there is and have found nothing in any of them to tell me how to handle horses on the ground." By this he meant general handling, such as haltering, leading, restraining, hoof trimming, grooming, and the many other things a person does around a horse when he is not actually riding him. The idea for this chapter grew from my friend's suggestion.

Let's start out by catching a horse that is in a pasture and doesn't want to be caught. This friend has pastures of some size but has no way to catch a horse once he turns it out. I'm always hounding him to build traps. Every pasture should have a trap. It is necessary if you need to catch an unwilling horse. One day I went to his place and helped him build one. We had his hard-to-catch mare caught five minutes after the trap was completed.

A good trap is easy to build. Posts with boards, poles, or woven wire comprise the materials. The trap should have two openings—gates, so the horses won't be permanently trapped if they happen to wander in. They can be fed in the trap to accustom them to it. It's generally a simple matter to place food in the trap and close the gates while the horse eats.

Five-foot sides are what I'd consider minimal. A low fence will only encourage a horse to try to climb or jump out.

Of course, a corral can be considered a trap. At Meridian

133

Meadows, for example, all main pastures lead directly into the corrals so that any horse on the place can be caught at any time. There are five corrals, two of which could be considered arenas. The smaller pens are used for corralling and catching horses.

The pastures at Meridian Meadows lead into a grassy trap about an acre in size. A large herd can be held in this trap for an hour or so. They are then driven into a 40-by-180-foot trap. Certain animals can be driven into a 40-by-40-foot catch pen. This trap is complete with snubbing post and colt chute. It's difficult to rope horses on foot in a big pen because a green colt will drag the roper all over the place. The small 40-by-40-foot pen is easy because the colt has nowhere to go but around. The snubbing post can be reached, and no horse in the world can loosen *that* snubbing post.

Handling horses on a big horse outfit is different from playing around with a few mares. It was impossible for us to take the time with colts that should be taken. When the stable sold some colts, we broke them to lead, then broke some others. Naturally, we always had some colts that didn't lead. They would have to be caught for shots, worming, and hoof trimming.

Previously, I'd forefooted, thrown, and tied down colts. This is hard on horseflesh and people. I always knock my hip out of place after throwing a lot of colts. The colts are frightened by this treatment, though I consider it easier on them than catching them around the neck and choking them down.

One year, with forty colts to work, we decided that some form of chute was necessary. We used our calf chute a few times but had some colts go over backwards and get wedged upside down. Only sheer manpower got them out.

The colt chute was built against a solid wall in the 40-by-40-foot pen. We couldn't build it high enough actually to contain colts because we had to have access to their necks for shots. The chute was about 5 feet long by 4½ feet high. The outside is both a gate and a wall. This allows us to turn a colt loose if he should get down in the chute. He can't get hurt in this little chute.

The front of the chute is padded with old inner tubes. A stout board up front is used to hold the colt down as a lead rope is snubbed to it. A wing leading into the chute is taken down when we're through working colts. It takes at least two men to work colts through the chute, because a colt will try to jump out when the gate is slammed on him. We had to figure out some way to contain the colt in this low chute and the following is our tried and true system. The colt is run in the chute, and the gate is shut on him. A man ready with a large blindfold with ear holes cut in it flips the blindfold over the colt's head. This keeps the colt down on the ground. Then a halter is worked on under the blindfold, and the colt is snubbed down. Shots can easily be given. We did forty colts in two hours in this chute.

If we want to trim hoofs, the same procedure is followed. The blindfolded colt is then led to the snubbing post. As mentioned earlier, a colt will seldom kick or fight when blindfolded.

Blindfolds and snubbing posts aren't used much in the United States, but both are used extensively in South America. Since many of our mares have always been restrained with a blindfold, it's silly to try other methods on them. They fight a foot rope until they're sore and exhausted but will stand for anything when blindfolded.

Some ranches in South America operate short-handed, as we do here. Their short cut is the blindfold. They have a *tapaojos* on the hackamore they use for colt breaking and even have the blindfold on the *jáquima* they use under the

135

bridle. It's a shock to handle one of their colts on the ground. You think you're saddling a lion if you try it without a blindfold. This rank creature is gentle and well reined when you're up. Their blindfold is pulled down over the eyes for saddling and mounting, then pushed up when the rider's ready to go. Most South American outfits have horses gentled better than this, but when they're man-poor, anything goes.

Catching a horse is sometimes a difficult thing to do. For instance, the horse is penned or stalled, yet won't allow a person near its head to slip on the halter. Heels are presented first. Few horses intentionally try to kick a person; most will simply whirl away, though they can knock you down by swinging away and hitting you with the rear end.

Many horsemen advocate "whip breaking" a horse that's bad to catch. This method is fine if it isn't overdone. One exponent of this facet of training, Captain Murrel Eddy, a friend of mine, was once showing me how to perform this useful part of training. He popped a little mare on the fanny, and she *put him out of there*. He came out minus his shirt. He wore her teeth marks for a long time. Folks, you better know your horse before you start spanking them with a whip.

Actually, you correctly whip-break a horse by lightly tapping him on the rear extremities, then petting or feeding the front end. Most horses soon learn to present their heads because it's more fun to get a tidbit than to get a spanked fanny. But even a light tap with a whip will annoy some horses and get them on the fight. A horse will surely kick at you, so use a long longeing whip. I hardly ever use any form of whip for any purpose.

I rope mares, colts, and any other horses that don't want to be caught. I've heard horse owners say that they'd fire any man they ever caught roping their horses. Many authors of training articles and horse books are dead-set against it.

136

A With the straight throw there is no swing over the head.

B The loop heads for its target.

C Note the follow-through. The slack is jerked. Many beginners try to jerk it with the hand that holds the coils. It should be jerked with the throwing hand. Here it is thrown quickly and hard, to keep the loop high.

The straight throw.

137

I've always thought that folks who are so much against roping horses are folks who can't rope.

You should never have metal of any sort on a lariat you
use for horse catching because you could conceivably knock
a horse's eye out with a metal honda. I use a regular tied
honda with a leather burner which takes the wear instead
of the rope.

I use three throws for catching horses around the neck.
The first—and the loop used most of the time—is the regular throw—one swing over the head and fire at the target.
This isn't a favored horse-catch loop, but I have worked
with many sharp horses. You can't catch them unless they run
past you. They'll stand in a corner, ducking the loop all day.
A regular throw as they run past means that they're caught.

The other two throws are regular horse-catch loops and
are executed with the palm of the hand up. I describe these
loops in the photographs and captions.

When I started working with Colombian Pasos, I thought
that they were the worst horses to catch I ever saw. A mare
in a stall was impossible to halter. I had to rope every one.
I saw how easy it was when visiting Colombia for the first
time.

The Pasos had always been roped. No one walked up to
a horse with a halter. Instead, the roper used a light *jáquima*
made of twisted rawhide with a twenty-foot lead line. A boy
would walk into a stall with his *jáquima* and throw it over
the horse's neck. The horse had been roped a thousand times
and would stand there and allow the *jáquima* to be put on its
head. It took about three seconds. We found that almost all
the Pasos stand when this ritual is followed.

A one-hundred-foot twisted rawhide *reata* is the common
Colombian tool, though a rope two hundred feet long isn't
unusual. I once saw a horse herd held on a grassy lot in up-

B The palm is up. The loop will circle the roper's head and then be released after one revolution.

A The loop is held to the left of the roper. He brings the loop around, to the back, with his palm up. This is a widely used horse catch.

C The loop is released, and the hand returns to its normal position. The hoolihan loop has a nice drop to it. Thrown well, it drops over the horse's head perfectly.

The hoolihan or dead loop.

139

A The hand is turned over when the loop is released, like the regular hoolihan, but the rope starts from the right. This is a more difficult throw than the straight throw.

B The California hoolihan has been thrown. The hand is returning to its normal position.

The California horse catch.

140

town Medellín. There was no fence at all. Two boys with long lariats walked out and caught any horse we asked to see. They made a loop and held about fifty feet of coils with the loop in one hand and threw the whole thing like a baseball. Those boys didn't miss. It was amazing to see that rope floating in the air, gradually nearing a running horse, and finally slapping down around the neck. They had to lead (throw ahead of) a horse a great distance. I tried their method and couldn't catch a post.

Roping a horse to catch it doesn't mean that you always have to keep it up. As the horse gentles and gets over its fear, regular methods will work. About a third of the brood mares at Meridian Meadows could be caught by walking up to them. But it saved time to rope them. When we gave shots, for instance, we worked on 140 animals at a time. I'd rope and lead to halter while a helper held the horse, blindfolded, for the vet. They'd do a horse as fast as I could catch one. I guess we averaged two minutes for each horse.

Gentling a horse so that you can slip on a halter is easy if you'll feed him from your hand. He'll expect a tidbit and will allow you to halter him easily if you make this a common practice.

I've expounded on the subject of hand feeding earlier. I favor it because I like friendly horses. Like the guy who went to the doctor, raised his arms over his head and said, "Doc, when I do this it hurts." The doc replied, "Don't do that." Hand feeding is like that. If your horse gets nippy or wants to walk all over you when you feed him a goody from your hand, stop hand feeding him, but don't condemn the practice.

Many horses won't let you walk up to them in a pasture if you carry a halter and they can see it. These same horses will follow you all around a field when you go out for a visit. You can catch such a horse by getting an arm around the

141

A The rope is around the horse's neck, and the end of the rope is held as shown.

B The fingers hold the rope with the rope's end still in place. The whole thing is twisted until a loop is formed.

The bowline knot is a knot frequently used around horses. This is the bowline variation which we find best for all our purposes. It's very important to learn to tie this knot quickly, so practice it!

horse's neck, slipping off your belt and leading the horse in with it. I often do this. A tidbit for the horse helps. I also go out and visit the horses, petting and scratching them around the withers, an especially itchy spot. This keeps them friendly.

A better practice than using your belt is to stick about ten feet of small-diameter rope in your pocket. Learn to tie a bowline knot. Tie the bowline around a horse's neck with your sneaky rope, put a half hitch over his nose, and come on in. A gentle horse can be led anywhere with such a rig.

How about a horse not so gentle? I don't like to see folks lead with just a halter. A long lead rope is much safer. Get out of the lazy habit of leading a horse by the halter; any horse might spook and hurt you because you're so close or at least jerk away from you. How many times have you grabbed the halter on a horse in a lot or pasture and had the horse jerk away from you? When you do such a thing you're

142

c The end of the rope is placed under the main rope and then is pulled a bit to lengthen it.

d The end of the rope comes back through the loop and the knot is made.

e The knot is pulled down in place. When one studies the knot, it's easy to see why it won't tighten.

teaching the horse *always* to jerk away when you catch him. Use a long, stout lead rope.

I fashion a halter out of a nylon lariat (or any old lariat). The rig is hard to beat as a halter. It's good because you can sit back and punish a horse if he's hard to handle—and the lead rope is so long that you're safe.

There are many methods of restraint which keep a horse from jumping around while you work on it. I favor some sort of hobbles on a spook and train every colt to stand in hobbles.

The easiest way to train a colt to hobbles is to tie up a

back leg and hobble his front ones. He can't go anywhere and soon learns to stand. Don't do this on hard or rocky ground. Sand or plowed-up ground or inside a good breaking pen is the right place. If the colt falls to his knees a few times, he won't be injured on a soft surface. I'd rather take the time to make a place to do this than give a colt a big knee for life.

Later you may wish to hobble a colt in front only. Something may spook him, and he'll learn to run on front hobbles. When this happens, I tie a rope to the front hobbles and dump the colt. A little of this goes a long way; it's strong medicine.

A good method of restraint is simply to buckle a strap on the front leg. Pick the leg up as you would to clean the hoof and strap it up. A strong belt with a lot of holes punched in it is perfect. Use a strong buckle and punch the holes big so that the strap can be easily jerked loose. This is a fine means of restraint to use on a mare during stallion service. It's hard for her to kick. We strap up the leg, wrap the mare's tail, wash her rear end, and bring up the stallion. When he has mounted and all has gone well, we slip the foot strap off and allow her to stand. Nothing could be simpler. Don't leave her leg strapped up for a long time. Fifteen minutes is long enough.

Colombians favor the snubbing post; I agree with them. I've seen few snubbing posts used in the United States, and I tell you all that there's nothing handier. It's much safer than crossties, a ring in the wall, or the top rail in your arena, because a bronc can trap you against a wall at any of those places. With a post you have a full circle—360 degrees—of escape when a horse blows up. When a horse is tied to a fence post, you have less than ninety degrees of escape route, and you can get hurt.

Since a snubbing post is an object by itself, with nothing

to support it, it needs to be big, heavy, and made of a wood that won't rot right off. We made the mistake of using a creosote post and were covered with creosote burns after working a large number of colts. It's O.K. to creosote the part that goes in the ground.

Soil is sandy here in northern Florida, so we set snubbing posts at least 4½ feet in the ground. The post is a foot through and stands about 5 feet high. A low post is no good because the colt will try to go over the top of it. A very high post is unhandy but is very good once the colt is snubbed to it. I've seen posts 8 feet high in Colombia. The usual post is 5 feet high and notched so that the rope won't slip down. I sincerely urge every person who works with many colts to set a good snubbing post in his bronc corral.

I suppose quite a number of people rope colts to catch them. I do. Still, you can spoil colts by not being able to hold them once you've caught them. You may think that you can hold a colt once you rope him, but you can't hold them all. When a colt learns to run directly away from you, digging in every jump, you can't hold him. The snubbing post can. I have worked with a few mares that would leave when roped; the post cured them.

The snubbing post can hurt you the same way dally roping can. You can get fingers, a hand, or an arm caught when you try to dally around a post. The safest method I've found is this: I rope a colt, and he takes off around the forty-by-forty-foot pen. When the rope hits the snubbing post, the horse starts a wrap. I duck under the lariat and go the other way. I now have a full wrap around the post and can hold the horse. A helper drives the colt towards the post, and I take up slack until the colt is close. We then either halter or blindfold very quickly before the colt chokes down. A colt broken to lead generally won't choke down. He'll come up

145

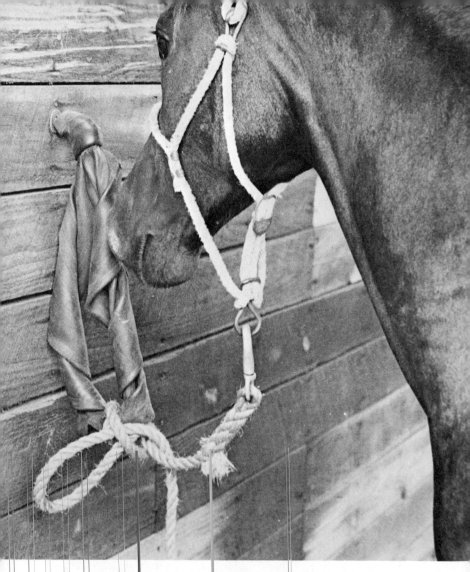

If a colt must be tied by his halter, using an old inner tube is a good safety precaution. The give in it makes it almost impossible for the colt to hurt himself.

when he knows that he's caught. A rank, unbroken colt will have a large blindfold flipped on his head. If he's too rank for this, I'll catch his forelegs and dump him. He's then haltered and snubbed to the post for education.

Crossties shouldn't be used for colts because colts often fight, get twisted up in the ropes, and quickly choke. It's hard to get to them to cut them loose because the action is generally fast and furious. Whenever you try to handle colts using the same facilities that you use for old, gentle horses, you're asking for big trouble. The bronc corral is the place for colts. Again, let me say that the bronc corral is about forty by forty feet—small enough for your rope to reach the snubbing post, which is set firmly in the center. It's high so a colt won't try to jump out. Eight feet is a good height. I once had a dandy post made of eight-foot slabs set upright. This may sound like a pen for wild elephants, but top facilities make colt training much easier.

I've said that a person who states that he never ropes his colts just can't rope. Sure it scares colts, but you have to get hold of them somehow. I'd rather catch a colt quickly than try for hours with the colt beating me at every attempt. They're not that stupid. I've seen many a four- or five-year-old horse that was out in a pasture, never caught, because the *owner couldn't catch him*. When you have something that big and old, you have a real problem.

So, how about learning to rope? I'll tell you how so that you can learn the fundamentals.

To start, roping an object without swinging the rope over your head is proper. Trail the loop out behind you and bring it forward with full arm and body motion. You may have thrown to the right or left, but you can correct for this. Try to use very little wrist. If the loop whips around and doesn't travel straight, you're using excessive wrist motion.

147

Coil up the rope from the end, not the loop. You'll notice that the lariat wants to twist, making it hard to coil. You'll have to keep turning the rope the way it wants to turn so that it won't twist. A few days of practice throwing and coiling up should make you a master of this.

You must learn how to pick up your slack. If you don't jerk the loop up after a throw, the colt will run through the loop or get too deep in it. Catching a colt around the belly means trouble. We sometimes catch a foot in the loop or even catch a quick one around the belly. For this reason, I always take two ropes with me when I have colts to catch. I can catch the colt again if my first loop was wrong.

A novice always jerks slack with the hand he holds his extra coils in because he misses his slack with the throwing arm. Practice reaching for the slack as soon as you throw. If you can keep a little contact with the rope (with the throwing hand) as it flies out, you'll find it easier. Good practice for this is roping the snubbing post. Try to rope it and jerk slack so that the rope only drops a foot or so down the post.

The rope is never whirled much in the horse corral. A whirling rope will spook horses, and they'll tear around, knocking each other down and getting all skinned up on the fence. One swing and a throw is enough. A horse can be caught with the straight throw, no swing. Then there are varieties of the horse loop, called *dead loops, hoolihans,* and so on. These throws all travel and drop in a different fashion. If a horse is facing one way, we'll throw a dead loop that'll drop on him correctly.

I have worked some mares that are impossible to rope when they're standing looking at you. They'll duck the loop every time, often accomplishing this simply by dropping their heads to the ground. We catch such mares by running them

148

past us. A swing, a throw, and they're caught. A few of these mares will run on a rope so they're caught in the small bronc corral with the handy snubbing post. If there is access to the corrals from every pasture, no mare is impossible to catch. True, I have often taken short cuts by roping mares in the pasture, but that's dangerous. In most cases time is saved and safety preserved by bringing brood stock and colts to the corrals to catch them.

Brood mares and colts, like all horses, need occasional hoof trimming. This isn't difficult if the animal has normal hoofs. We'll illustrate hoof trimming photographically. Actually, all there is to it is to trim off excessive growth of the wall of the hoof. The ragged pieces of frog are trimmed, but the frog itself is left intact. The bars of the hoof should never be cut out because they greatly help keep the hoofs from contracting.

Some old mares resent having their hoofs trimmed, and they must be restrained. There are many methods of restraint which I'll go over. Many horses have been made bad to trim and shoe by hair-triggered horseshoers who fly off the handle and beat up a horse at the slightest provocation. Don't let such a person on your place.

Many mares can be restrained by using a blindfold or twitch. This is simpler than tying up hoofs because when a horse throws a "whingy" while he's tied up and you're trimming, you can easily get caught, trapped, and hurt. If you have to tie up legs for hoof trimming, have an experienced person help you. When you're trimming front hoofs, tied or strapped up, you need help to pull the hoof out away from the horse to give yourself working room.

The illustrations show you how to tie up a front hoof, step by step. This is a safe way to do things. There are few that can't be trimmed with the front hoof up. Naturally, you can't

149

A The front hoof has been picked up and is being inspected prior to trimming.

B The sole has been cleaned with a hoof knife, and the area near the wall of the hoof has been evened to show where the nippers will cut the wall.

Trimming the hoofs.

150

c The extra high wall is cut away.

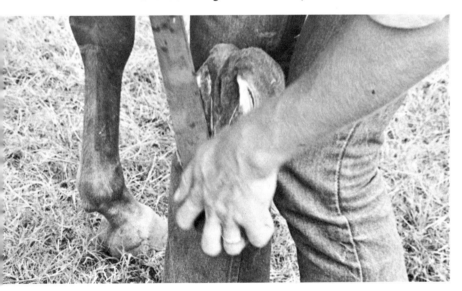

d The rasp evens up the work and is the final step in hoof trimming.

151

A Once you can tie the bowline knot, you can use it to Scotch hobble a mare that needs doctoring. One safe way to do this is by using an old cinch with the tongue and the material that holds the cinch together removed so the cinch can be spread apart.

B One cinch ring is passed through the opened cinch.

The Scotch hobble and the bowline.

do a beautiful job when you must use such methods, but excessive hoof growth must be trimmed away.

A back hoof can be drawn up in a Scotch hobble. The horse can't kick backwards but can still reach forward. He can't use much force, though, when the hoof is already a foot off the ground.

A hind hoof can be drawn up by braiding or tying a large ring in the tail. A heavy strap is buckled around the pastern and a rope snapped or tied in it. The rope is then run through the ring at the tail, and the hoof is drawn up. The rope is finally tied off at the ring on the strap around the pastern. A horse can be trimmed and shod easier this way than by using a Scotch hobble. How do you buckle the strap on the pastern? How do you tie the ring on the tail? Simple! Scotch hobble the other hind leg.

Many a rank old mare will fight forever if you try to tie

152

c Now run the foot rope through the cinch ring. The mare can't get a rope burn now.

d The foot rope is passed under the neck rope.

e Tie off. You can now doctor the mare without any fear of getting kicked.

up any of her legs. There's only one way to handle such a horse. Throw her, tie her down, and fly at it. A helper can hold her legs off the ground by means of a separate rope. A pole can be pushed under the tied legs, run over the body and the legs are held up by leverage.

How do you throw such a mare? It's a rough job, fellows, and your ol' mare may get a few rope burns, but she must have her toes trimmed once in a while. Maybe once or twice a year is enough for such a wild one.

There are few horses I can't Scotch-hobble. Any really experienced bronc fighter can Scotch almost any horse. A long heavy soft rope is used to minimize rope burns. When

153

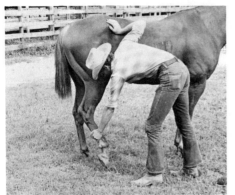

A Place the right hand on the horse's hip. Ease the left hand down the leg to get a firm hold. Leverage makes it difficult for the horse to kick.

B The hoof is picked up while the man moves into position.

The correct way to pick up a hind hoof.

that hind hoof is picked up, the end must be run through the neck loop quickly. I twist the rope several times between the hoof and the neck rope, run it through the neck rope, and draw up the rope. If they fight, the rope must be hitched quickly. When they stop fighting, I Scotch the other hind leg. This pulls the horse into a sitting position. The next step is to push the horse over on its side and securely tie the legs with a soft rope. If you have good, sturdy Utah hobbles, you can hobble the left hind to the left front, right hind to right front, and tie your hobbles together. This is pretty foolproof. But watch those hoofs when you're tying the horse down. They can still reach out, and the punch from a hind hoof is terrific when the horse is lying on the ground. A really big help is to have someone with strong hands grasp the flank skin firmly because this more or less paralyzes a horse. This method also comes in handy when you're turning the "torpedo" loose.

154

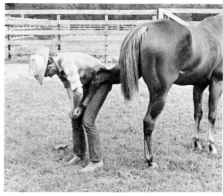

c The hoof is *eased* over the man's leg. If the horse kicks, the man can easily step away.

D The hoof in the final position, being trimmed by a hoof knife.

I have worked with a few mares that were almost impossible to Scotch-hobble. They fought so stupendously that they'd seriously rope-burn themselves if they didn't kill the whole crew in the process. We did trim their hoofs, and I know of only one way without calling the vet to put them to sleep. I forefooted the mare, threw her, and a helper jumped on her head and held her while I tied her down. This is rough and should be attempted by only the most experienced bronc fighters.

Many people make the mistake of being too firm with a stallion. They expect instant obedience from the horse during service and often get this obedience. If a horse acts up they whip him. Any little mistake means that the stallion gets whipped. I think that a horse will tolerate just so much of this sort of treatment and no more. Sooner or later the stallion will turn on the mean handler, injuring or killing him. The stallion has tremendous power and will use it against an enemy, be the enemy another horse or a hated handler.

I never whip a stallion, favoring the idea of making him

155

my friend. The stallions at Meridian Meadows came when I called them. They liked me. If they tried to take advantage of our friendship, I'd slap them, but there were no whips there. If a horse gets rank I'll throw and tie him down, but I won't whip him. I'll tie a stallion to a snubbing post and make him stand there for an hour or so, but I won't do this when it's hot or when flies are bad.

Don't expect 100 per cent obedience in breeding season. You don't have perfection in people, so why expect it from horses? When we bring a stallion up to a mare, we have him on a twenty-foot lead rope rather than on a short halter shank. A snug hackamore protects his handlers and the mares from his teeth. He can be jerked back with the hackamore and long rope if something goes wrong.

Many people fuss over a stallion too much. The horse resents being bothered all the time. A stallion is generally quick and a bit mischievous. Visitors often want to go into a stallion's stall or exercise lot, stand there, and talk. The stallion will soon come up and be a bother. So the stallion's handler will slap him, an action the horse resents. It's a better plan to get the people out of the horse's area and then talk.

When I ride a stallion, I don't spend all day grooming him. If he's really dirty a quick bath is better than rubbing him for hours. I saddle him and go on. When the ride is over, he's washed and put up. In other words, I don't fuss with him because I know he'll fuss with me if I do.

Books have been written about brood-herd management, but I'll include here a short section on my own observations.

I think a mare should be at least three years old before being bred. I've seen two-year-olds that were thrown out of balance so that they didn't even come in heat as three-year-olds. I've seen others that came in heat and never went out of heat all season. This is the result of hormone imbalance, and I'm sure one cause is breeding immature fillies. Also, a young filly needs special care and feeding to grow and develop while carrying a fetus.

Mares can have a hormone imbalance at any age. Those easily fattened "easy keepers" seem especially prone to imbalance. At Meridian Meadows mares with this problem are given Follicle Stimulating Hormone (chorianic gonadotrophic hormone). My little Paso cutting mare, Yocunda, was fat inside, and we never seemed able to get her settled. She was extremely nervous, as are most mares with a hormone imbalance of cystic ovaries. We finally settled for regular FSH shots, and she soon was heavy in foal and her change in disposition was remarkable.

I have never seriously delved into the problems of trying to get a very large number of mares settled. Many mares have serious hormone and ovary trouble which keeps them from being settled. A by-product of this problem is extreme nervousness. This seems to answer some questions I've had about mares, many of which I've considered "screwballs" in the past. This is one reason why most riders prefer geldings. A mare with a hormone imbalance and (or) cystic ovaries is going to be almost untrainable because the trainer can't cope with these problems.

So, if you have a nervous flighty mare that has proved to be a trainer's Nemesis, please have her checked out by your veterinarian.

This same hormone is also valuable for stallions. By the time our old stallion, Mahoma, was thirty-three years old, we had managed to get fourteen mares bred to him before he quit, losing interest because of his extreme age. This horse was far too valuable to forget because of his remarkable con-

157

formation and natural Paso gait and because he was a terrifically strong and potent sire.

So we gave Mahoma a hormone called testosterone. It gave him the urge but not the ability, and we got no mares settled for eight months. Finally we went to FSH, and Mahoma started to respond. He also received wheat-germ oil and some pills that stimulate spermatozoa. Mahoma was ridden daily and turned out in a grassy lot after his ride. Soon he looked and acted like a young horse.

I'm beginning to think that a mare about to be served should act a certain way and has something wrong with her if she deviates from the norm. The only "abnormal" acts that seem to be sort of normal are "silent heat" mares. This type of mare must be roughly teased by a stallion before showing any sign of being in heat. If she kicks and squeals, she's out of heat. If she silently stands there, perhaps glaring at the stallion, she's in heat.

The normal mare shows signs of being in heat by exhibiting great interest in a stallion. She'll tease easily, urinate and back to the stallion spraddle-legged, with her tail held high over her back.

The cystic, fat, or imbalanced mare will show signs of heat but will squeal and kick at the stallion. A cystic mare will often be constantly in heat, always endeavoring to ovulate but never being able to.

We began following the practice of examining a mare to find out about when she's ready for service. Since heat periods are abnormally long in the early spring, an examination of the mare proves to be a great saving on the stallion. I've been doing this for several years and am still no expert at it. A good veterinarian should be able to tell you when the mare is ready.

The method we use for this is to insert a clean plastic tube into the vagina and examine the cervix by inserting a special flashlight through the tube. The cervix loses its tight look, appearing flaccid and dropping down near the bottom of the vagina when the mare is ready to ovulate.

Some mares have normal heat periods all year, but this is very rare. Most are dormant during the winter, having a very long heat period in early spring and settling down to normal heat periods during the spring and early summer. In July and August periods may last only a few days. The amount of daily sunlight is said to have a direct relation to the mare's heat periods. It's also said that heat periods can be regulated by providing artificial light, such as a lightbulb in the mare's stall.

I learned years ago, that a good bronc pen, a lariat, and foot ropes were far superior to special chutes for handling horses. A breeding chute is just something to cripple a mare and trap a stallion. Get a mare fighting in a chute and you have more than your share of trouble.

Build good traps and corrals, and many of your troubles are over. Use a snubbing post and hobbles. And, when you get in deep water and can't swim, call lifeguards, who, in this case, are your vet and professional horse handler.

XIV *The Tail End*

This is a chapter of odds and ends, much of them based on questions people ask me. A lot of advice comes from my observations about correct and incorrect horse handling.

Gear

Many people have little or no idea where to get good horse gear. Novice horsemen generally buy worthless junk— bridles that are no good, saddles that fit neither horse nor rider, blankets that wrinkle, and odds and ends that they have no use for. Any product pertaining to horses seems to sell, so the market is constantly being flooded with worthless stuff.

Though I've tried to make my words clear, some people still think that when I write about hackamores I mean those darn, junky, worthless hackamore bits. I don't own a hackamore bit. If I had one around, I'd go right out, dig a hole, and bury it.

Again let me describe a hackamore. A hackamore is the English derivation of the Spanish word *jáquima*, which simply means "noseband." It is made by cutting thin strips of rawhide and braiding them over a *rawhide* core. Most hackamores are braided over cable cores. Such hackamores can't be shaped. They always retain the shape they have in the store. Since I shape my hackamores to fit a horse's jaw, I use only hackamores braided over rawhide cores or those braided with no core at all.

160

Getting a good hackamore is becoming increasingly difficult. You can buy the noseband, headstall, *mecate*, and *fiador* from several outfits.

Jack Carroll, of Carroll Saddle Company, mentioned earlier, isn't interested in making any cheap horse gear. Rather, he favors the working cowboy. He makes good hackamores, good bits, and fine saddles. I can vouch for anything coming from his shop.

Strange as it may seem, I often ride an English saddle when this type of gear is called for, and you'll find English bridles hanging in my tack room. The English saddle I favor is the Passier, a dressage saddle I bought from Miller Harness Company. This is a good company to deal with. They carry about anything a person needs around a stable and will send you a big catalog.

I also purchase gear from H. K. Kauffman & Sons Saddlery Company. You can't go wrong with either company.

Windy Ryan has a fine western line in his store, Ryan Saddle and Ranch Supply. When I want a top lariat, I think of no one else. If you ride a conventional stock saddle, you won't be disappointed with what you order from Ryan's.

I'm not really plugging these companies for any return. It's just that I get a lot of mail asking where good gear can be purchased.

One more word about saddles. Make sure that your saddle is wide enough for your colt. You can always pad a rig that's too wide, but you have no recourse with a narrow rig that pinches. Try a few saddles on your horse, and tell your saddle maker if you need an extremely wide rig.

Feeding

I recently read that we know less about horses, horse care, and feeding than we knew fifty years ago. Yet we now have

161

all manner of feeds to choose from. They contain food, minerals, vitamins, and all sorts of ingredients. Nutritionists say a horse needs them. Yet I've had horses look and feel as good on crimped oats and bran as they do on a mixed horse feed. There are more supplements on the market than I can think of. I'd say, roughly, that they're about the same in quality. I believe vitamin A is more stable in a powder than as a pellet. A feed supplement is good if it isn't overdone.

I once attended a lecture by a prominent equine practitioner, the head of a large veterinary college. He said that he visited a breeding farm where nothing but grass was fed. No supplements were given. The horses had all kinds of leg deformities. He suggested a supplement, and soon normal colts were being foaled. This outfit needed supplements.

Then he visited another horse farm where the owner bought all kinds of supplements and used them. He was having as much leg trouble as the other outfit. The veterinarian suggested cutting off most of the extras, and soon normal colts were being foaled.

The gentleman then said, "You ask me whether supplements are necessary and I tell you that I don't know. They are good in some cases and do more harm than good in others."

I once worked for a ranch in South Dakota and noticed with alarm that foals were coming with bad deformities. Bowed legs and knuckling pasterns were common. My first move was to ask a good veterinarian about the troubles.

That section of the country was deficient in phosphorous, so we checked the formula of O. R. Adams, the top vet at Oklahoma State University, for a way to correct this deficiency. His book *Lameness in Horses* said that a ration of three parts phosphorous to one part calcium was required.

162

We were using a high-phosphorous mineral supplement but it contained 27 per cent calcium and only 10 per cent phosphorous. So we were daily adding to our problem.

The next order of business was to fortify our mineral mix. We acquired straight phosphorus and brought the balance up to three to one. The mares ate the supplement, and the necessary phosphorus traveled via milk to the foals. In a manner of a month all the colts and fillies were perfectly straight.

The moral of my tale is that supplements at first made our condition much worse but that eventually the correct supplement cured our afflictions. So, it seems to me, the indiscriminate use of supplements is wrong, and your expert, your veterinarian, should be consulted.

Worming

Some people never worm their horses. Others worm them all the time. We now have so many wormers on the market that it's total confusion knowing what to use.

It was different twenty years ago. We wormed horses once a year, after the first hard frost. We had carbon disulfide capsules for bots and phenothiazine for bloodworms and roundworms. After treatment some horses would get down, moan and groan, and feel terrible for a while.

There are all kinds of wormers today that you just put in your horse feed. I guess that they work all right. Horses are generally wormed and then wormed two weeks later to get the eggs. I'd say worming four times a year is enough. Horses must be wormed more often in warm climates than in regions where hard freezes are common. If I lived in Montana, for example, I'd worm horses in November and worm no more until the next November. My favorite worm medicine is Parvex, and my favorite method is to have a veterinarian administer it with a stomach tube.

163

Stabling

Meridian Meadows has ideal conditions for stabling a horse. A horse has a twelve-by-twelve-foot box stall which opens into a twenty-four-by-one-hundred-foot exercise run. Hay is dropped into a manger from above. A grain cart is pushed down the aisle and is put into grain drawers. All this saves time. A forty-stall barn is fed in a manner of minutes.

The barn aisle is fourteen feet wide so that stalls can be cleaned and bedded down with the aid of a truck or tractor and manure spreader. Automatic fly-spray dispensers expel a minute amount of spray every fifteen minutes. All in all, it's a very good setup.

The working arena is covered but has no sides because the great problem in this region is heat, not cold. There is a watering system to keep dust down. A fine feature is the availability of the arena—the barn and arena are one building, end to end. I like this better than having stalls lining the arena. Horses can be worked while other employees are cleaning stalls. No hay and bedding gets in the arena. This is the best system I've ever used. I find no fault with it.

This arrangement isn't as automatic as it sounds. Waterers must be inspected because the horses will often foul them with droppings. Many horses will take grain to the waterer and drink. Food in the waterer soon gets rank. And when the power supply fails, wow! But it beats lugging water to all those horses.

The hay drops are fine, but if the boys get careless, they'll feed one horse too much, another not enough. And droppings fall in the mangers, too. Many horses appear to take dead aim at a manger. Automation is fine, but inspection is necessary!

This situation could only be more ideal by having each

stall open into a pasture. That's impossible with such a great number of horses. But if you have a couple of horses, such an arrangement is ideal.

I don't believe in keeping horses shut up in a stall unless they have good daily exercise. Nothing is worse for man or beast than total lack of exercise. It's like solitary confinement.

Meridian Meadows goes to extremes with exercise. Studs are even run together until they're long two-year-olds. The Colombian horses are very sensible about this. They play and fight but seem to grow and develop in fine shape. Don't do this on my say-so. You might get a fine colt hurt. The colts at Meridian Meadows have been playing together since they were foaled. Don't *you* turn a stallion out with another stallion. Raising them together is one thing. Turning a strange stud with another stud can result in injury or death to a fine horse.

Brood mares are never in the barn unless they're injured or sick. Colts foal in a special pasture which is inspected regularly. Mares that are having trouble get help. When a real problem arises, she's kept in a little isolation barn. There are eight stalls there with three grassy lots. Any horse can be easily driven into a stall.

The pastures are checked daily. This is necessary because horses can find dangerous objects to get caught in, poisonous weeds to eat, and all sorts of objects to get cut on. One mare was lost in a forked tree. She was scratching her neck and got hung up. A filly caught her front hoofs in a split tree, broke both legs, and died of the pain. We cut down all the forked trees and boarded up splits.

A top filly, bent on suicide, caught her neck in a two-inch gap between gate and post and choked to death. We filled all such gates. A top colt managed to tangle himself in a fence composed of seven taut, smooth wires run through posts.

We were there in minutes to rescue him, but it took months for his full recovery. Such problems arose even when pastures were checked daily. Some people turn horses in a pasture and forget them for a year.

One time a mare foaled a month early. She was out with open mares and with mares not quite ready to foal. Those mares without foals do their darndest to steal a young foal, and that mare must have had hell all night fighting off her girl friends.

Don, my rider, caught the colt, and the mare was all over him. He fought her off with his hat until I roped her. Together we fought off the mare until we made the gate. This mare got a good day's rest in the barn and then was turned in with mares with foals.

Loading and Hauling

Most people trailer horses too fast, whip around turns too fast, and stop too quickly. A good suggestion I heard is to ride in your own trailer and try to stand up without touching the sides for support. Of course, it's illegal to ride in a trailer on a highway, but try it in a pasture or a rough lane. You'll learn a lot.

It's a wonder that a horse will go into a trailer at all after having been hauled very much. You can help him by driving defensively on the road. Slow down in advance and give the horse a little signal in advance. Turn your wheels a bit to move the trailer *before* turning. This way the horse can wake up and get set.

I think it's a good idea to tranquilize a horse that doesn't get hauled much. It's far better (and cheaper) to have your vet come out and administer a tranquilizer than to have a dangerous fight with a good horse.

The show horse that is hauled all the time must learn to

166

be loaded and hauled without drugs. The best way I know of to get a horse to like a trailer is to feed him in it. If he knows he'll get feed when he walks into the trailer, he'll load willingly.

Take the trailer into his lot if possible. Block it so that it won't move when he enters. Show him feed and fool around with him until he goes in easily. Leave the trailer there and feed him in it for a week or so. When you want to haul to a show, feed him hay or grain every time in *his* trailer. Drive the right way, and hauling shouldn't be a problem.

Now we all know that this is the way to do it, but how many people actually take the time and trouble to allow the horse to like a trailer? Mighty few. This extra effort will pay off. I suggest it, recommend it, and sincerely ask you to make it.

O.K., how do you load a horse that's almost impossible to load? I favor one system above all others. Two soft ropes are ideal. Tie one to the trailer side and one to the trailer post in the middle. Bring up the horse. He has a lane he must stay in because a man is holding each rope. Another man keeps the horse facing the trailer. The men work the horse up near the trailer and exchange ropes. Each man can take a wrap around the trailer brace posts if this is needed. Almost all horses will load in this fashion.

What if a horse kicks, jumps, rears, and so on? Run him up a ramp into a stock truck. He has no business in a trailer. If you have to either haul him in a trailer or feed him to the foxes, throw and tie him down. This, plus a tranquilizer, should let you haul him.

At one ranch I managed we once had a bronc mare brought to us for stallion service. She was so wild they had her hauled to us with a load of roping calves. She was eleven years old and would barely load. She had to go home in a trailer.

We tried everything. Nothing worked. She reared, denting

167

the trailer top. She bucked, kicked, and had a regular fit. I finally threw her and tied her down. She stayed down for two hours. When I untied her, she meekly entered the trailer with no trouble.

Getting Along with Other Horsemen

It seems to me that all real horsemen should have a common bond, a love of fine horses. This isn't the case. English riders feel that the "cowboys" are crude and know nothing about the finer points of equitation. Western riders wouldn't be caught dead on a "flat" saddle. Each could learn a great deal from the other. Being a good fellow is a help. Keep your mouth closed instead of criticizing others, and the world will be a more pleasant place. Find something to admire about other forms of horsemanship and mention it. Bread cast on the waters has a way of returning. It's a lot easier to like a person who's complimentary. If you like a person, he'll like you. In this way a better feeling is gained all the way around.

I like Thoroughbreds and enjoy watching them run. The handlers really know how to care for a horse. They have to because it's their business.

Standardbreds pulling those little sulkies always make your heart beat doubletime. It's a thrilling sport. No one knows more about a horse than a top Standardbred man. They're a fine bunch of fellows. Drive a Standardbred and you're in for the thrill of your life.

I personally can't get too warmed up about Tennessee Walkers or Saddlebreds because I wholeheartedly disagree with weighted, abnormally long hoofs and tails that are cut and set. I think this is the height of cruelty brought on by vanity. But I love dressage horses and have picked up a lot of training knowledge from my friends who are exponents of dressage and high school horses.

I don't ride hunters and jumpers, but I do enjoy watching them. I like these horses and the people who ride them. There's nothing there for the western advocate to fault. These are gritty people—it takes know-how and courage to ride a hunter or jumper. You have to be good to do it at all.

I hope these few words about different types of horses and riders helps a little to unify horsemen.

About Trainers from a Trainer

Some people must think I'm an awful hypocrite. I say that rough trainers are no good and yet detail such methods as throwing a frightened colt to leave him tied in the hot sun. To a person who raises fine Thoroughbreds, my methods of colt gentling would seem far too rough. I heartily agree. The Thoroughbred owner spends thousands of dollars on a fine colt and *expects* a good return on his money. If he pays sixty-five thousand dollars for a colt, he certainly won't throw that colt and tie him down. He'll hire enough help to gradually gentle him and keep him friendly. The slow, patient way is always the best.

People who raise pleasure horses have to pay help at least the minimum wage. Everything costs a lot except horses. The government lurks, ready to leap on the small breeder and put him out of business. And taxes—wow—enough said!

Pleasure-horse breeders must work short-handed to come out at all. Short cuts must be taken. I don't feel that short cuts are necessarily cruel. Common sense dictates what's cruel and what isn't.

Get a rank fresh colt to handle and you must be able to get your hands on him. It might take months of getting acquainted before the colt would allow the halter to be slipped on. So I don't believe that roping the colt is cruel.

Then you must be able to brush him, pick up his hoofs,

169

and saddle him. If you have him tied to the fence, he'll set back, rear, and jump all over you. He'll hurt you or himself. Restraining him with hobbles allows you to handle him. He'll gentle in half an hour. Then you can really get after him.

Now suppose the colt's tied to the fence. He kicks you in the leg and you lose your temper, grab a whip, and almost beat the life out of the colt. You can gentle him that way, but you remove his spirit and make a zombie out of him. And, it's just plain cruel.

You'd be surprised at how many rank colts come to a trainer's barn. The owners have tried them and spoiled them. They buck, rear, kick, bite, and run away. These horses are handled in different fashions. Many "trainers" just fly at them with a club. We throw and tie the man-haters down, go all over them with our hands, sack them out, and leave them tied down to think about it. We never beat a horse. We never whip a horse. Soft ropes or straps restrain them, and blankets under their heads keep sand and trash out of their eyes and ears. They feel our hands, and soon learn there's nothing to fear. They can't run or fight so they give up. The horse is changed.

When I was a kid, I broke a half-Arabian filly for a lady friend of mine. The filly was very mischievous but certainly wasn't rank. She'd "crow-hop" a little, then go on to enjoy the ride.

The lady was pregnant. A week after her baby was born she decided to go for a ride. She placed an English saddle on the filly, bitted her with a Weymouth bridle (both snaffle and curb bits), and got on. She lasted one jump and was hospitalized for a month.

The filly, during the lady's stay in the hospital, was taken to a farm for care. The farmer's son tried the filly, and she put him down. The farmer got a hame strap and whipped the spirit out of the filly. She was finally sold to a riding stable as a spiritless plug for anyone to hack around on. She was a zombie.

The *real* old-time cowboy was and is rough, but he never broke a horse's spirit. Some of these modern rough-and-tough boys do. You can't beat a horse into gentleness without breaking his spirit.

Tying a colt down and hobbling him allows a trainer to get his hands on a frightened bronc and show him there's little to fear. The youngster can't get away or fight, so he must pay attention to his lessons. If you have time, by all means take the slow route. But don't whip him.

I think a trainer's methods should be investigated before you take a colt to him. Drop by and watch him work. If he's really a rough one, he won't be able to contain himself too long. Many a rough trainer is successful and has winners and champions to his credit, so the choice is up to you. A horse can fear and dread a man and still win for him. It's your horse. Personally, I like friendship from a horse.

So cruelty is relative. I guess it's more cruel to keep a horse in a tail set than it is to knock on a cutting horse. Breaking a Thoroughbred as a yearling and running him as a two-year-old seems pretty mean because it generally cripples the colt, but at least he's well fed. When you see a fellow break a two-by-four over a horse's head and see other people pet and kiss a horse infested with worms and underfed to the starvation point, you have to wonder if ignorance isn't the cruelest thing of all.

Index

173

174

INDEX

175